to Bob — A g[ood]
mentor and teacher
stay strong for our
students. They are
our future.

God Keep you
and your family

5/7/07

A Parenting Guidebook

The Roles of School, Family, Teachers, Religion, Community, Local, State and Federal Government in Assisting Parents with Rearing Their Children

by

Dr. Willie J. Kimmons

authorHOUSE™

1663 LIBERTY DRIVE, SUITE 200
BLOOMINGTON, INDIANA 47403
(800) 839-8640
WWW.AUTHORHOUSE.COM

First published by AuthorHouse 04/26/06

ISBN: 1-4208-1340-4 (sc)
ISBN: 1-4208-1339-0 (dj)

Library of Congress Control Number: 2004099367

Printed in the United States of America
Bloomington, Indiana

This book is printed on acid-free paper.

A guidebook with useful strategies and recommendations for parental involvement in the growth and development of children

Table of Contents

Dedication

This Parenting Guidebook is dedicated to my six special grandchildren, Ashley Michele, 1 year old, Layla Paige, 2 years old, Kendall Nicole, 2 ½ years old, Lauren Bacall, 4 ½ years old, Aaron Malik, 6 years old, and Sean, 10 years old. This next generation represents our future.

WJK

Willie James Kimmons

Acknowledgments

This guidebook represents the work of many people in our day care centers and Pre-K-12 schools across this country. It includes the parents, grandparents, family members, friends, teachers, administrators, school support staff personnel, parent-teacher associations, religious leaders, political leaders, community leaders, federal government, and the children (students) we serve every day. Various groups shared information on how they perceive their role and how they promote parental involvement.

Special appreciation and thanks to Mrs. Ruby Jefferson for her tireless efforts, collaboration and the invaluable support in typing numerous drafts of this manuscript. Thanks to the many writers who granted permission to use their work that have authored articles and books on rearing children. Invaluable information was used from the fact sheets on parental and teacher involvement produced by the United States Department of Education and the National Parent Teacher Association. Thanks to the number of proofreaders and editors who read the drafts of the book.

Foreword

As a former director of New York City Day Care Centers and now a retired educator and politician, I realize the importance of this guidebook for parents. It is a well known fact that when parents, grandparents, teachers, administrators, politicians and communities all work together, schools get better and students get the high quality education they need and deserve to lead productive lives. Quality education is paramount to a child's growth, development and success in life. Education is about discovering the special talents and skills of our children and guiding their learning according to high standards.

Parents are the necessary key ingredients in improving children's education. It is imperative that schools and day care centers across America do a better job of reaching out to parents and grandparents. From my experience in day care education, parents want to help their children succeed in school, and often need guidance on how to be better parents for their children.

This parent guidebook is designed to assist parents in understanding the connection of their role and the role of all the agencies and community groups who are there for support. This book is to help parents and families to become more active participants in their children's education. To make sure that no child is left behind in our educational system, this timely and much needed guidebook has excellent suggestions and recommendations for helping parents and families get involved. I encourage all interested educators, parents, grandparents, community leaders and concerned citizens to read this guidebook.

The Honorable Shirley Chisholm
Former Director of New York City
Day Care Centers, Retired Educator,
and Former Member of Congress

About the Author

Dr. Kimmons was born in Hernando, Mississippi. He was reared in Memphis, Tennessee where he attended public schools and received his high school diploma from Frederick Douglass High School. He was a student athlete and received an athletic scholarship to attend Lincoln University in Jefferson City, Missouri. While at Lincoln University, he was active in the Student Government Association and ROTC. He served as a First Lieutenant in the United States Army, Adjutant General Corps, during the Vietnam era as an Administrative, Data Processing, and Personnel Officer.

Dr. Willie J. Kimmons received his Bachelor of Science Degree in Health Education and Psychology from Lincoln University in Jefferson City, Missouri, Masters of Science Degree in Curriculum and Instruction; Doctorate Degree in Education Administration and Supervision in Higher Education, both from Northern Illinois University, Dekalb, Illinois.

Dr. Kimmons has served at every level in the higher education teaching and learning process with dedication and distinction. Over the past thirty-seven years, he has been a Classroom Teacher (Sikeston Middle School, Sikeston, MO), a Program Director (Central State University, Wilberforce, OH), Assistant Dean (North Carolina Central University, Durham, NC), Dean (St. Francis College, Brooklyn, NY; the University of the District of Columbia, Washington, DC; Fayetteville State University, Fayetteville, NC and Gaston College, Gastonia, NC), Vice President (Lawson State Community College, Birmingham, AL), Interim President (Trenholm State Technical College, Montgomery AL), President, Downtown Campus Wayne County Community College, Detroit, Michigan, and Chancellor (Ivy Tech State College, Bloomington, IN). Currently, he is serving as an Educational Consultant for Pre-K-16 schools, author, and as a motivational speaker. Dr. Kimmons' consultant work focuses in the areas of Title I programs, parental involvement, teacher and administrative training, management, budget development, strategic and long range planning, collective bargaining, contract negotiations, human resource development and stress management for public schools, two and four year colleges and universities.

He has given more than 500 presentations and lectures to all types of organizations including educational associations, Chambers of Commerce, universities, two and four year colleges, high schools, middle schools, elementary schools, day care centers, head start groups, churches, religious organizations, Kiwanis, Rotary and Lions clubs, NAACP, Urban League, economic development organizations, political groups, Greek organizations, youth groups, parenting conferences, workshops, and other community organizations. Dr. Kimmons has served as nationwide spokesperson for diabetes, breast and prostate cancer, and health related matters and he serves on the African American Men's Health Summit, Steering Committee for Central Florida. He is a member of the Volusia and Flagler Counties African American Men's Prostate Cancer Board of Directors, Daytona Beach, Florida.

Dr. Kimmons is Vice-Chairperson of Daytona Beach Community Relations Council; Board member of Daytona Beach/Volusia County Association for Retarded Citizens; Board member of Daytona Beach/ Volusia County Health Department; Vice President of the Volusia County Florida (MAD DADS) Men Against Destruction-Defending Against Drugs, and Social Disorder, and Facilitator "Young Male's Rites of Passage Program", Greater Friendship Baptist Church, Daytona Beach, Florida, Board member of the Daytona Beach/ Volusia County Salvation Army, and Vice President, Volusia County Florida First Step Juvenile Residential Facility.

Dr. Kimmons' interest in higher education stems from a background of training and experience in the area of human development, leadership and community service. He is always eager to promote learning and development of the student by setting the atmosphere to motivate not only the student, but also all individuals within the student's educational arena.

Dr. Kimmons was the 2003 recipient of the <u>Futhering Rights, Investing In Equality And Nurturing Diversity (F.R.I.E.N.D.)</u> Award in Orlando Florida. The Florida Civil Rights and Human Relations Commission honored him for his outstanding mentoring and volunteer work in public schools.

Dr. Willie J. Kimmons has spent his entire career getting to the root of and understanding the nature of today's students' issues. He has successfully dealt with many of the challenges of today's student throughout his career as a professional educator. His life's ambition is to promote the survival and progress of education, and continue his commitment and dedication to the learner.

Introduction

"Knowledge is Power and No one can take it Away from you "

About this book...

This book is intended to assist parents and others who are involved in the important job of helping to raise and educate children. Children are our greatest resource; they are our future and an extension of parents. Having quality parental involvement in the early stages of a child's life is crucial and paramount to the growth and development of successful adults.

What is the basic problem that faces parents today? Some parents say the lack of financial resources and the inability to spend enough quality time with their children are real concerns. The responsibility of all parents is to help their children develop in a way that will equip them to function well as individuals, family members and good citizens. Parents are most able and willing to do this when they, the parents, have a sense of belonging and importance in society. This sense of belonging can only be felt when the rights of parents are protected and obstacles to earning a living and respect are not placed in their way. Belonging to the whole provides individuals with a sense of security. A sense of belonging makes it easy and right for parents to understand and accept the values and ways of the society and pass them on to their children.

Educators know that parents are children's first and most influential teachers, and must help and encourage parents to be actively involved in their children's education. Our schools simply cannot do the job alone! Parent institutes, conferences, seminars, workshops and parental training programs are made available to help educators provide the information parents need to get involved and stay involved as active members of the home-school team.

Research findings of Child Psychiatrists/Psychologists and educational leaders, in Pre-K-12 education show that to build reading abilities, children must want to read (Comer & Poussaint 1976). Unfortunately, many children aren't interested. Most often, television, video games, overly busy schedules, socializing or listening to music simply distract children. The motivation just isn't there, no matter how important educators say reading is. Parents can make the difference, probably better than anyone else. They can show children that reading is fun and rewarding. This book will explain how. It also provides ideas to further motivate children who already love to read. Parents will learn that when they motivate children to read, they also motivate them to learn. Motivation improves school success more than anything else. Reading is one of the most important keys to learning. If children read well, chances are they will do well in school.

Reading is and should be, undoubtedly, a top priority for teachers in our schools around the country. But without the help of parents, studies show that many children will not achieve their highest reading potential. Parents who encourage reading by having reading materials available for children, set a good example for reading at home; and having family conversations about books can make a huge difference in the achievement of their children. Getting parents on the school's team in the nation's schools to improve reading skills will enhance student achievement—and schools' test scores. Reading is the foundation of school success. No matter what a child's age, research proves that parents, grandparents, relatives and friends can all play an important role in school success in building needed reading skills. Parental involvement is crucial if students are to achieve their full potential in life.

It is never too late for parents to make a difference. Research clearly shows that children denied adult care, support and guidance function poorly in school and may suffer irreparable damage that will handicap them throughout their lives. The educational impact of such parental neglect, however unintended, is devastating. Thousands of concerned educators tell us, "Parents don't have the basics of parenting." Parents need all the help that they can get. We can address this pressing problem by working together as parents, teachers and concerned citizens. Children learn by exploring. Children learn by observing. Children learn by doing and this is what good parenting is and should be. In this book, we will explore some of the avenues to improve parenting skills and to get more parents involved in the lives of their children. It will list many agency roles in assisting parents, grandparents, school officials, relatives, friends and other concerned citizens in raising and teaching children to learn. There are a number of strategies in this book for parents to use in assisting their children to be productive in life.

A good home learning routine gives everyone a chance to succeed. There is no one right way to do it. The routine itself should be designed to provide a feeling of accomplishment. It gives parents and grandparents a chance to step back and children a chance to step forward. The idea is to help parents, grandparents, and children feel good and get to know each other better in the bargain.

For this parenting guidebook, I am listing the 100 ways for parents to be involved in their children's education presented by the National Parent Teacher Association in Washington D.C. 2002:

1. "Give positive feedback and show appreciation for teachers and principal.

2. Approach interaction with a positive attitude and an open mind.

3. Listen to others' viewpoints.

4. Share your child's strengths, talents, and interests with your child's teachers.

5. Share expectations and set goals together with your child.

6. Make appointments as needed to discuss your child's progress or concerns.

7. Attend parent-teacher conferences with specific questions you want to ask.

8. Indicate the best way to give you information (telephone number, e-mail, notes).

9. Understand and reinforce school rules and expectations at home.

10. Participate in informal opportunities to talk with and get to know school staff and educators.

11. Address concerns or questions honestly, openly, and early on.

12. Attend PTA or parent meetings regularly.

13. Read classroom and/or school newsletters.

14. Visit your school's web page.

15. Know your staff's extensions and office hours.

16. Read and know your school's handbook.

17. Request that information be available in all relevant languages.

18. Share your family's culture, values, and parenting practices with your child's school.

19. Share your perception with educators and school staff of how parents are treated.

20. Work with school staff and educators to revise and improve perceptions and school climate.

21. Meet your child's friends and get to know their parents.

22. Contact your school for information on family programs and resources.

23. Help establish a parent center at school and use its resources.

24. Help create a toy/book lending library and visit it regularly.

25. Assist in developing parent support programs/groups and attend them.

26. Attend workshops or seminars on various parenting topics. Participate in parenting classes on child development, expectations, discipline, etc.

27. Attend parent fairs and other events especially for parents and families.

28. Start a parent book club to discuss current publications.

29. Help create and/or contribute to a school newsletter on parenting.

30. Assist in creating and/or offer your services to before-and after-school programs.

31. Build a child file with medical records, picture, fingerprints, etc.

32. Make donations and/or offer to work at clothing drives or swaps, food co-ops, etc.

33. Talk with your child's teacher for ideas on parent/child games and activities.

34. Discuss your child's school day and homework daily.

35. Learn your child's strengths and weaknesses in different areas of school.

36. Provide a quiet, well-lighted place with basic school supplies for studying/homework.

37. Help your children break down projects into smaller, more manageable steps.

38. Develop a consistent daily routine and time for studying and homework.

39. Provide encouragement and approval for effort and schoolwork.

40. Share your interests, hobbies, and talents with your children.

41. Provide children with books, magazines and so forth, and develop a night time reading routine.

42. View selected television programs together and then review and discuss them.

43. Make family trips to the library, zoo, museum, or park a fun learning experience.

44. Talk with your child's teacher on creating home learning games and activities.

45. Complete interactive homework assignments with your child.

46. Attend meetings on learning expectations, assessment, and grading procedures.

47. Help set goals and develop a personalized education plan for your child.

48. Participate in activities that help you understand school technology.

49. Help plan and attend family nights on improving study habits, doing homework, etc.

50. Help develop, or offer services to your school's study/tutor center.

51. Participate in fairs and tests for math, science, history, and so forth.

52. Respond to school surveys on your interests, talents, and skills.

53. Let school staff know your availability to volunteer (days, times, and how often).

54. Supervise and coordinate evening and weekend volunteer activities at school.

55. Assist your child's teacher in the classroom or on field trips when you are able.

56. Work with school staff and teachers to develop volunteer activities you can do from home.

57. Assist school staff and educators in creating a warm and welcoming atmosphere for parents.

58. Help provide childcare and/or transportation for volunteering parents.

59. Help develop creative ways to use volunteers at school.

60. Actively help school staff recruit parents and community members as volunteers.

61. Attend training and orientation on how to be an effective volunteer.

62. Learn and uphold school discipline, confidentiality, and other policies as a volunteer.

63. Plan a regular time each week to talk with school staff and educators with whom you are working.

64. Help develop volunteer job descriptions and evaluations.

65. Participate in organizing and planning ways to recognize and appreciate volunteers.

66. Respond to school surveys /questionnaires on how effective volunteer programs are.

67. Help develop and distribute a volunteer directory to parents, school staff, and teachers.

68. Provide volunteer consulting services to school staff or educators on your areas of expertise.

69. Learn of school and district policies and practices that affect children.

70. Voice your support or concerns on any issue that will affect your family.

71. Be involved in decisions on student placement and course and textbook selections.

72. Participate in meetings to determine special educational needs and services.

73. Attend workshops on problem solving, conflict resolution, public speaking and so forth.

74. Serve on school advisory councils or committees on curriculum, discipline, and so forth.

75. Serve on a site-based school management team with teachers and the principal.

76. Encourage and support older children in serving in student leadership positions.

77. Help your school create a student's rights and responsibilities guide for families.

78. Attend PTA, school board, and/or town meetings and speak on issues of concern.

79. Learn representatives' backgrounds and participate in school board elections.

80. Work with teachers and school administrators to develop a parent involvement policy.

81. Write, call, or travel to state capitals to support or oppose proposed legislation.

82. Participate in petition drives or letter-writing campaigns to Congress on legislation.

83. Give testimony at public hearings in support or opposition to education legislation.

84. Vote in local, state, and federal elections for public officials who support education.

85. Help your school develop a directory of social and community services.

86. Find out information on community resources and organization and use them.

87. Help develop and/or distribute a community newsletter to local agencies and businesses.

88. Help coordinate and participate in an event to raise money for a local charity.

89. Talk with employers about holding parent meetings/workshops on site.

90. Advocate for flexible work schedules and leave time to attend school functions.

91. Encourage employers and local businesses to make donations and support school programs.

92. Help organize and/or participate in community health fairs.

93. Help recruit community members (seniors, business people) to volunteer at school.

94. Become active in community groups such as YMCA and Boy and Girl Scouts.

95. Serve on local community advisory councils and committees.

96. Work with local authorities and public officials to sponsor community events.

97. Help organize and/or participate in a community "clean up or beautification" project.

98. Encourage and help facilitate your child's participation in community service.

100. Be a role model, be active in community service yourself or together with your child."

Children naturally look to important adults in their lives as models of what they should do. They want to please and to imitate important adults. Obviously, parents and teachers are important adults to them.

That means if you want your children to work hard on school subjects, you have to demonstrate in your life that school learning is important. You have to seek answers in books, show curiosity about math facts, or indicate that it is important to you to learn what is going on in society and in government, for example, in order to vote wisely.

You can do those things by asking questions out loud and then asking how you can find the answers, "I wonder if there is a way for me to learn how to use a computer? I could look in the newspaper for an ad that might give me information." Then you can pursue answers in newspapers or encyclopedias or call the library for help. There are all kinds of ways of demonstrating to your children that you are curious about the world and new knowledge. This helps your children want to achieve similar attitudes and skills themselves.

Be enthusiastic about learning - your child will be, too.

Children generally want to please their parents and their teachers. They will respond well when those important adults praise them and occasionally reward them for their efforts. When your children ask questions and pursue answers by looking them up in the dictionary, newspaper, or magazine, you ought to say: "Hey, that's a smart idea. Now you're thinking. You're going to do well if you keep that up."

Parents, when your child talks about what is going on in school, you can show interest and enthusiasm for what the child is learning. Naturally, you want to praise a child when she is making progress. That doesn't mean waiting until the child brings home a paper with an "A" on it. If a teacher says your child is doing better this week than last week, or better this report period than the last report period, that's a time for rejoicing at home. Then you can say, "Way to go! Now you're working. I'm sure glad to see that you are improving. That's just ...

Praise is one of the best motivators of all.

Parents, one of the best ways to motivate a child to do school work is to show that it has application outside of school. For example, can we parents show that reading stories enriches our emotional lives? Can we demonstrate that math is used regularly in our shopping, our check writing, and our measuring to buy paint for our walls? Can we find information in newspapers and magazines that helps us decide how to vote, how to plan a trip, or how to solve a health problem? It takes effort and attention to those kinds of details for us to help children see that what they are doing in school will pay off in life. It's all part of a well-known principle in psychology: the more visible and real we can make something, the more likely it is that we will achieve it.

Help your child use lessons learned in school at home.

We said that the goal has to be visible. It's even more important that the means to achieve the goal are clear and concrete. One of the reasons many of us don't achieve our dreams is that we have no sense of how to move from where we are now toward the dream.

I can remember one little third-grade boy writing about his dream to be a professional basketball player like Magic Johnson. In his composition he said that all of his friends, teachers, and parents thought that he would never be like Magic Johnson because he was too clumsy and not fast enough. He said that it was awful when no one believed him. Wouldn't it have been wonderful if some of those people had given him some direction? Wouldn't it have been uplifting for that child if his parent had said: "If you're going to be like Magic Johnson, you are going to have to learn to run fast and to shoot well. Why don't you start by shooting baskets after school every afternoon or by getting on a local Boys' Club track team to run faster?" By giving him steps to take, the parent would have allowed the boy to keep his dream at a point in his life when encouragement and support were so important.

Motivation for children is not just interest, and it is not gimmicks that simply catch their attention. Motivation means focusing on a goal and laying out clear steps needed to achieve that goal. Parents play an extremely important role in helping children become motivated for school work. So, first, be a model of curiosity for your children. Second, praise and reward them for their efforts to learn. Third, help your children solve practical problems according to what they have learned in school. And finally, always help your children take the first little steps that lead them to bigger goals. Then you'll be surprised at how motivated your children will be in school.

Help your child see that there are ways to reach even the biggest goals.

The general thought in many instances, is that schools are not preparing a large number of the youth population for a fruitful contribution to the society in which they will have to live. Educators are too preoccupied with change. Many individuals will attest to the fact that there is rampant confusion in the pedagogical world with respect to goals, objectives and how one pursues said purposes via the existing educational mechanism. Individuals who have had successful teaching experiences by deviating from the traditional norm often find themselves discounted by "professionals." These successful teaching experiences will not work, according to the traditionalists, because they are inapplicable in an "educational context." Many refuse to see that most changes in school curriculum result in students being expected to learn a variety of irrelevant superficialities which is why a majority of students understandably do not become enthusiastic in their courses. Apparently, this approach is devised to show the world that educators can "keep up" with progress, but sadly it bears little relationship to the needs of the progress that is happening in the real world.

Progress in our society has always emanated from individuals who have somehow learned to think things out for themselves and thus to do things they have not previously been shown by someone else. Nobody showed Mr. Alexander Graham Bell how to make a telephone; Mr. Thomas Edison how to make a light bulb; Dr. George Washington Carver the importance of the peanut; or Mrs. Shirley Chisholm how to be a Congresswoman.

Our schools seem to inhibit the process of "personal discovery". Inventiveness is totally strange to teachers or the majority of them. They seem more interested in maintaining an authoritarian stance.

Teacher training is predominantly an extension of the same faulty method that prevails in the schools: a set of classes in which an authoritarian professor or teacher stands in front of a class of students teaching them from a syllabus that becomes even further removed from the reality of today's world.

In the view of many of today's educators, teaching and learning are completely separate and almost unrelated activities. Teacher teaches. Students learn. Good teaching can help learning happen but it is not the teachers' fault if students do not want to learn. We beg to differ: all the good teachers we have known were good because they could induce in their students the desire to learn.

Although there is widespread unemployment there are jobs going begging in trades where the rate is as high as seven dollars per hour. The jobs remain unfilled and our educational system has to share some of the blame for this set of circumstances. It is quite clear that training to meet the needs of a highly automated and technological society is not being accomplished in many of our educational institutions.

Education in the early years of our republic was for the privileged few who could afford the time and expense, rather than for those who formed the backbone of the laboring classes upon which this nation was built. While the schools were Americanizing the children of the European immigrants, they were ignoring the children of those other immigrants, who were brought here by force—the African slaves.

Today it is well past the time for the public schools to move out of the 19th century and into the 20th... and indeed... the 21st century. Our system of education may have met the needs of society then, but it has not been capable of meeting many of the current needs in our society. Parents of the children of today are totally different from what they were 40 to 50 years ago.

The early notion that education was for the elite no longer makes sense in a society that demands that every worker not only be able to read, write and add two and two, but must also adapt to a highly technological work-force. The ultimate extreme in this trend occurs when a poorly educated product of our public school system is required to pass a civil service examination in order to become a janitor, a street cleaner or hospital worker.

To put it bluntly, society has outdistanced the schools at a hare's pace while public education plods along like a turtle. The change will come by using the turtle's superior cunning and determination so that the schools can gear up, speed up and get back out in front of the hare. No one has a greater stake in urging that turtle on than the minority groups who have traditionally been cheated in this race!

Directly related to this, I believe is the situation we are faced with in attempting to combat the problem of dropping out in our educational system. The "inferiority myth," formerly given as the primary reason for the dropping out of black students, has been exposed. We should realize that it is not merely the lack of interest that causes students to leave school. Dropping out is not merely the inevitable result of a student's individual personality hang-ups. Facing reality will enable us to see that the problem is the sense of futility that the students experience, often subconsciously.

Why should one remain in school until one becomes the recipient of a diploma when it is apparent that the student is in no way better prepared to cope with the outside world? When in reality, the individual is in no way more capable of understanding life. To the dropout, an education in terms of public schooling is irrelevant, that is, not meaningful to what is seen and understood about the world. We must demonstrate to all students that there is a very real reason for being in school. The real reason to attend school is to be educated and empowered to escape low income living, high unemployment, poor health care, and inadequate housing.

What, I believe, is needed is to realize that our education structure is too large, too insensitive, and too out of touch with the unique problems of the various communities within each of the major cities to be able to deal with them effectively. American culture is not a culture of homogeneous values. When we attempt to indoctrinate a system that is not thrown open to all of us, we attempt to reinforce through school systems social values basic only to one segment of our population. It can only result in a sense of frustration, hopelessness and rage in those who have not had the benefit of the "system's" values in their pre-school experiences.

In discussing alternatives in the educational realm, community control can be the vehicle by which school and community become as one, and by which teachers, now transmitters become developers, advocates of the system and of the student. It can be the vehicle by which parents now spectators become participants. Progress is rarely made where the views of those who are involved have no impact, where the persons who guide and control activities are not amenable to our sanction. This is the situation that so many parents, students, and even teachers, find themselves in today. They have no real voice in policy because those who are in charge of making policy, are too far removed from the decision making process. We must localize the structure of the school system and permit the administrator and teacher to be answerable to the immediate and pressing needs of the community they serve rather than to the far removed desires of those who sit above them.

There must be no fear in thinking through alternatives in education; tradition is no longer the answer when the results indicate the most negative set of responses. Education must indeed adapt a most crucial attitude if they are to deal successfully with Black students and students of color. Some educational critics believe that inner city schools often hamper the full development of Black student's intellectual capacity. Inferior facilities coupled with less personal attention to his/her progress often renders the Black students unable to present the high school academic record which measures one's full capacity for intellectual growth. What we desperately need is a breed of educators with the courage to admit that our huge and expensive system of higher education was built on a design that is about 98% out of date. In addition, we need a system that has the appropriate personnel with the right amount of energy and vision to start rebuilding itself into a system that has meaning for today's society.

Alternative models of education are already in use: high school equivalent exams are available to the ambitious drop-out; night schools offer collegiate education; proprietary (i.e. profit making) schools offer training in a large number of technical skills. Employees have both formal and informal training programs, and some sponsored educational programs for executives and workers. Man-power training programs have become a major government activity in the past decade and are widely touted as the remedy for poverty and excessive welfare payments.

Individuals involved in alternative educational concepts must view the learning process as something more than an academician passing on knowledge to a captive learner. Then the professor examines the learner to determine the extent to which one has retained what was intended to be learned. In several of the alternative education models, the student rather than the subject becomes the center of the learning situation. Learning is an individual matter, and when the opportunity is there for the student to choose from a variety of learning experiences that are suited to the learner's needs and capacities, mastery quickly occurs. Learning occurs best when motivation and interest are internal!

If alternatives in the educational arena spark a few rebellious fires and it means breaking with routine teaching techniques that no longer seem to work, then so be it. As William Pierce, former secretary of HUD (Housing and Urban Development) has said "whatever will stimulate in students an appreciation of the learning process and a new confidence in their own ability is certainly worth a try."

Some General Characteristics of Alternative Schools:
- Innovative curriculums
- Positive school climate
- Small class size
- Flexible internal structures
- Constant staff development
- Strong links with outside communities

- Clear academic mission
- Strong academic leadership
- Diversified roles for teachers
- Increased participation of students in policy development activities.
- Strong support from parents and community.

It doesn't really matter what teaching and learning alternatives one takes as long as "real and relevant" teaching and learning takes place. Therefore, the activities outlined in this book set the format for learning to rear children all through life. The book suggests different ways that children learn and the role we all play in this learning process.

Chapter 2

The Role of Parents in Rearing Children

"Save Our Children, Save Our Schools, Never, Ever Give Up on Our Children"

Dr. Margaret Crosby, a retired professor of Education at Clemson University, Clemson, South Carolina in a parenting speech June 1, 1995, Jacksonville, Florida titled "A Child Becomes What He/ She is Taught By Careful Planning, Setting Goals, and Dreaming". She noted to a group of parents, that they are probably wondering, "Why they should become involved in their children's education?" Education experts widely agree that parental involvement has the following benefits:

1. Parental involvement leads to improved student performance.
2. As school activity becomes a shared experience, parents become closer to their children.
3. Parents find that they do have the skills to help their children to learn.
4. Relations between home and school improve.

Both teachers and parents are powerful role models and educators for children. If we work together, we can ensure that our children will have positive learning experiences both in and outside the classroom (Crosby, pp. 1& 2).

We are living in some very difficult times as it relates to the growth and development of our children. We as parents must do all that is necessary to make sure that our children have the best and most up-to-date education that this life can offer. As a grandparent and parent of four children who are now young adults, a career educator, classroom teacher, college administrator, a workshop presenter and motivational speaker at numerous parenting conferences and seminars, I can truly say that I have had extensive experience/ training in the area of parenting.

One of the most important facts I would like to stress in the area of parenting is that research tells us that all children are different and progress at different rates of development, therefore, their individual needs for learning and developing might require different methods, procedures, and techniques toward learning. They all have basic needs but some might need more attention than others. There are three standard modalites of learning:

1. Kinesthetic-touching and feeling
2. Auditorial- hearing
3. Visual- seeing

Therefore, parents and teachers remember, children learn differently, please keep this in mind. Research also tells us that the formative years are the most important years in terms of a child's ability to learn, grow and develop. Therefore, between the ages of birth and six years, it is most important that parents are aware of children's daily needs. Those needs are to be <u>loved, respected, nurtured</u>, and the exposure to a variety of experiences and activities. It is most important that we as parents be there for our children at these stages of growth and development.

We need to talk to our children. Many times, as infants, they don't know what we are saying, but they can hear and relate to the tone of your voice and they know that it is the parent's voice. Sing to the baby, this makes for a calming atmosphere. Listen to your children, especially a crying baby or child. That baby is not crying because he/she is spoiled. Most of the time the baby needs or wants something. The same with children, as they continue to grow and develop, first grade through high school, we as parents need to take the time to listen to our children. Sometimes it maybe something very simple and unimportant to us as adults, but it could make a world of a difference with the way a child feels. If we don't talk and listen to them at home, then they think that it is ok not to talk and listen at appropriate times at school. Most parents are working parents and are tired when the day is over, but in order for us to make sure that our children's needs are met on a daily basis, we should give our children some quality time. It might be only fifteen or twenty minutes to sit down and ask them questions like "How was your day at school?" "What did you read today?" If a child brings home a "C" or "D" grade, this is not the time to scream and hollar and say, "you should have done better!" Let's take the time to find out why and give the child some help and assurance that he/she can do better the next time. Then map out some strategies which would be helpful.

Parents always try to provide a quiet place in the home for your child to study, concentrate, and think and this does not mean with the television or the radio, DVD players, or cell phones. This is something we must teach our children that they must take time to **read**, **study**, and **enjoy a good book.** Parents should provide materials for their children, give them books for gifts, take them to the library, get your membership cards together, and let them see you read sometimes. Parents can be a powerful influence on their children's interest in learning to read. Current research bears this out. Reading experts agree that parents can make a crucial and positive difference in their children's educational progress just by reading to them. Despite this fact, current surveys indicate that only 35% of children age 3-8 are read to regularly by their parents- only 1/3 of America's parents regularly read to their children according to the National Center of Education Statistics, 1992. This is very important in the early development of our children. Parents, let me remind you that we need to be positive role models for our children. Usually they will do what they see us as parents do. If they don't do this, it is our responsibility as parents to teach them study habits and work habits at home. This home training will then transfer to the classroom and to later life.

We all know that it is important to be visible at our children's school. As soon as possible go and meet your child's teacher, attend PTA/PTO meeting and conferences, serve on the PTA/PTO board, and other school committees. When your child and your child's teachers see that you are interested then they become more interested and tend to work better together.

Ask your child's teacher to send home progress reports, let them know that you are interested when your child is doing well, as well as when there is a problem. This is crucial information to have as a parent, even if the parent can't read or write. Parents, get a church member, neighbor, friend, or family member to assist you with your child/children's schoolwork. In addition, these are some suggested ways for parents to motivate their child/children to learn:

1. Be a model of curiosity
2. Praise and reward efforts to learn
3. Solve real problems
4. Lay out the steps to success

Don't be intimidated by the school or the teacher. They are there to help you and your child. If you as a parent don't know how to help your child or don't understand what they are doing, ask questions or let the teacher know that your child needs extra help. Parents, this nothing to be ashamed of. Provide your child with a variety of instructional games and materials at home. You can make a game out of something as simple as cooking dinner. Everyone can be involved in talking about what's for dinner, writing and reading the recipes, planning the menu and taking care of chores like setting the table properly. Try to have one meal at the table with the whole family present at least once a week. This is when you can teach etiquette, table manners, and talk about the day's experiences or make plans for the next day. This is very important in teaching children how to communicate at home and this will carry over to the school, community, and life.

It is very important us as parents to instill within our children a good self-concept. They need to feel good about themselves and what they do and know that in order to achieve in life, they have to first, set goals, work hard and believe, then they will achieve and become successful individuals. Success breeds success. In order to instill within our children positive self-esteem, we need to praise them when they have done well. It can be for something small. These small praises will soon become big. We need to say things like, "I like the way you said that ", or "What a great story you wrote in your speech class today".

Let your child know that he/she is the most important person in the world and that you love him/her dearly. We need to make it a habit of smiling and giving many big hugs to our children. Even though we are smiling and giving hugs, there is always a time for discipline. This must be adhered to. This begins very early in parenting and children will understand what is expected of them. Most of all, be consistent and a good role model.

In loving our children we have put too much emphasis on material things, to try to give them what we did not have. In doing this, many times we are falling by the way side and forgetting that the most important things in life that we can give our children are love, moral values, a sense of responsibility, hard work and self-respect.

A good education is vital for our children today to succeed in life. Without it, many of them will be lost, on the streets, addicted to drugs and other crimes. With good consistent parenting skills and working very closely with the principals, counselors, and teachers in our schools, your child will grow up being well adjusted, well prepared, self confident and ready to take on the challenges of the world and become the great leaders of tomorrow.

Parents who care are always seeking to find effective ways to help their children to develop in a manner that they should. The question, "How do you want your child to be?" is often asked. Parents consider the following suggestions:

- If you want your child to be happy, provide him/her with an optimistic and challenging environment.

- If you want your child to be respectful and tolerant, provide him/her with a model who shows respect and tolerance for the child, others, and self.
- If you want your child to be independent and responsible, provide him/her with tasks appropriate to his/her age and interest level for which he/she is expected to do.
- If you want your child to learn, be a learner yourself and become knowledgeable about your parent-teacher role.
- If you want your child to have a positive self-concept, provide the child with tasks that the child can successfully accomplish and give praise for the accomplishments.
- If you want your child to be trustworthy, be honest in your parent-child relationships and indicate the desirable outcomes of honesty and integrity.
- If you want your child to relate to others in a positive way, be a friend to your child and provide him/her with opportunities to interact with his/her peers and adults.
- If you want your child to be able to cope with frustrations and disappointments, let him/her learn naturally and early through his/her own experiences.
- If you want your child to be cooperative, plan activities which require family members of friends working together.

Parents, a child becomes what he/she is taught by example and careful planning.

In order for you, the parents of today, to rear our future leaders of tomorrow, to be more effective citizens, you need to exert the following:

	More	Less
1	More positive feelings towards yourself and your children.	Less negative attitudes towards the school and other people.
2.	Talk more about ideas and ways of helping your children to have a bright future.	Talk less about others, unless we are saying something good about them.
3.	Talk more about what you can do for your children, community, home, and school.	Talk less about what our schools or community have not done for you.
4.	Talk more about what you can do together as parents.	Talk less about what "I have done".
5.	Work more with teachers, staff, and principals, to improve the quality of education for your child.	Talk less about what the teachers, staff, and principals have not done for you.
6.	Offer more encouragement to your children, the school, and other parents.	Less criticism of others in the school and community.
7.	Set high goals and expect better things for yourselves and your family as well as others whom you love.	Stop being limited in your future thoughts by the limitations of the past.

In Maureen Botrie and Pat Wenger's book titled "Teachers and Parents Together," 1992, their thoughts on parental involvement were by asking the question, "Why parental involvement?" They noted that greater positive parental involvement in education, through the school system and at home, may be the strongest single factor to promote student success. Educators need to help parents recognize their importance in positively impacting children. A parent who consciously exhibits a positive attitude toward education shapes his/her child's attitudes towards school and potential future success. A child's attitude and perception of school drives his/her work habits, attention and potential outcomes. If children see a home/school support system in place, it helps them to feel secure, directed, and confident.

Parents have a vested interest in seeing their children succeed. Preventative models can be applied in both home and school when parents become stronger guides for their children. If we don't help parents understand how to support their child's learning, we affect equity of outcomes in education. Some of today's complex, fragmented, busy families need the school to offer guidance, direction, and support. The school is increasingly becoming the preventative model, and the corrective nucleus for the community it serves.

Supportive empowered parents make a teacher's work easier. When parents view the school's climate as "inviting," they become good public relations advocates for that school. Parents also offer educators important information about the local community and individual children. This information provides teachers with knowledge that influences teaching. Schools need parental support to provide active, enriched programs without the cost of additional educational support. As well, many school programs require parental investment and involvement in order to be successful, for example: home reading programs, homework policies, and values education. An adversarial parent group can create a negative force, effectively canceling out the good work educators do with students.

Parents and teachers need to recognize the fact that they both have a positive, supportive role to play. Parents and teachers acting negatively toward one another do not build a healthy climate for children. Schools experiencing difficulties may want to clearly define what roles parents and educators play in order to lessen explosive reactions to issues from both parties. Everyone involved with students will be more rational, and coeducational support will be restored. To continue to enhance the role of parents in rearing their children a number of initiatives have been written. One is: Beyond the Bake Sale by A. Henderson et al. (National Committee for Citizens in Education, 1986) that promotes parental involvement and is written from a parent's perspective. It identified five hierarchical levels of parental involvement:

1. Partners - parents who fulfill the requirements for children to be involved in school successfully, that is, send their children to school on time, offer bedtime routines, provide appropriate dress, and nourish children adequately, respond to communications with the school, and so on.

2. Collaborators and Problem Solvers - parents who actively deal with home and school issues and work to solve and identify problems in collaboration with the school.

3. Audience - parents who appear at school to view a performance of one class or the whole school.

4. Supporters - parents who work in the school as parent volunteers.

5. Advisors and Co-decision Makers - parents, who help teachers to shape policies, hire staff, and so on.

The roles may not be as hierarchical as listed above. Each role has a value depending on the needs of your school. If your school needs parents to become more informed about routines, attendance, basic parenting, and so on, "partners" is the area on which to focus. If your school needs parents to become tutors and/or goal setters for children then focus on "collaborators". These kinds of parental involvement have direct impact on an individual student's school performance.

In schools where good public relations are essential, encourage parents to respond as an audience and as general school supporters. Schools that need extra hands in the classrooms and throughout the school to run their active programs would bring parents in as "supporters".

If parents and teachers are interested in shaping policies, you may need to decide where to cooperatively direct your energies first. We suggest addressing areas that directly impact parents and teachers, for example, a homework policy.

It is also possible for different committees and individual teachers to be addressing these levels in various ways at the same time; schools are complex, dynamic organizations that perform different functions simultaneously. However, schools that have carefully considered the needs of the families should be able to determine an appropriate direction.

Parent education or group meetings offer greater numbers of parents the opportunity to understand current education. If parents are invited to the school early in the year so that programs can be explained as simply and concretely as possible, they will develop a more realistic view of the school and its goals. It is important to recognize that all parents have been a part of an education system and therefore have their own views on education. Whenever possible, explain the curriculum to large groups of parents as this saves teacher energy and time.

Education has undergone many changes during the past decade. Parents need to understand the rationale for those changes before they will support them.

Before a new initiative is taken, consider how it will be perceived by the parents involved. Educators will benefit by stepping back and viewing change from the parents' perspective in order to diffuse possible conflict.

Parents also need to be honored by the school, especially those parents who directly contribute their time to its success. When you honor the parent, you honor the child. This is particularly important when dealing with inner-city families where culture between home and school may be very different.

Schools must not be afraid to stand by their principles about learning when an issue with an aggressive parent arises. Some parents will use the school as a target if they are undergoing stressful experiences. School policies offer strength to educators and help to create clear messages. When all potential solutions have been assessed and a compromise on a critical issue can not be reached, parents could possibly consider changing schools. Educators who experience similar stress could also consider this option.

Parents may need to be involved in the educational process before, during, and after a program implementation. If a program will directly affect parents in any way, they should be involved in shaping it. When a program requiring parental support is in place, their feedback should be used to modify or continue its direction. Parental evaluation of meetings, new reporting procedures, and so on offers educators a view on what parents find most useful. Schools also need to have in place a process where parent groups can access staff meetings when issues overlap roles. Parents and teachers can problem solve around particular issues. If schools "see" parents as having a legitimate voice, they will become more responsive to, and responsible for education.

It is natural for parents to talk about the school and their child's education, even when schools are not part of their conversation. Schools must accept this reality. If we make our schools inviting and promote a healthy interaction between teachers and parents, we have an opportunity to influence the tone of their talk.

Assessment/information about individual children needs to be given to parents in a specific, concrete, ongoing basis. The more information (e.g., writing folders) we collect throughout the year, the more we have to share with parents. If difficulties should be addressed, share the information with the parents early in the school year. Collaborative problem solving between home and school will help to create positive solutions. Parental support can be the crucial catalyst.

Videotapes of classroom programming and special events offer parents who cannot visit classrooms insight into school curriculum. Parents will get a clear idea of a classroom and their child's perception by watching a video. Most families have a VCR available, so videos should be used by schools to deepen understanding.

Many children become more actively involved in learning when they realize their parents will be viewing their performance.

Some students see their parents as wielding negative power within a school so they can then see themselves as powerful, negative forces. Teachers may be reluctant to deal with these students appropriately as they wish to avoid an aggressive parent. However, if these children are not dealt with at school fairly, their development becomes limited. This is not the outcome parents ultimately want.

Parents should be included in their child's celebration of learning. If we look for ways to invite parents to the school at the culmination of learning experiences, children have a supportive audience and parents have a real opportunity to view their child's learning. One of the most positive messages to children occurs when they see parents and teachers talking constructively together.

Programs offered within a school that help develop parents' knowledge can have a direct impact on the children they serve, especially inner-city parents, families new to the culture, or parents experiencing parenting problems. Parenting, computer, and literacy programs can support whole families.

When thinking about parents, we need to remember that all parents are individuals with their own views, experiences, and attitudes. We must respect this and not paint all parents with the same brush, especially if we have had negative experiences. Parents must also be reminded to see teachers as unique individuals with different teaching styles and strengths. The common threads between teachers and parents should be their interest, advocacy, and support for children (Botrie & Wenger pp. 9-13).

According to The Parent Institute Quick Tips, Fairfax Station, Virginia, (1995 & 1999) parents are teachers too! From the day children are born until they graduate from high school, they spend just 15 percent of their waking hours in school. The other 85 percent is spent outside of school–and most of that time is spent at home. That means that parents are their children's most influential teachers. Fortunately, children are naturally curious and love to learn (The Parent Institute 1995 & 1999).

Roles of Parents and Children

According to Botrie & Wenger (1992), there are specific roles of teachers, parents and children. Listed below are the roles of each:

Role of Teachers

Botrie and Wenger stated that parents and teachers play a crucial role in developing children. Together they provide a supportive safety net with which children can grow both at home and at school. Both groups are human and basically imperfect, so it is important that we work together to provide the most consistent support we can. Children also have responsibilities in the home and at school.

Role of Parents

1. To tell their children that school and education are important, as they will copy parents' viewpoints;
2. To remain supportive of the school in front of their children;
3. To treat the teacher with respect because she/he is the teacher;
4. To approach the teacher first if difficulties arise;
5. To listen to the teacher's point of view;
6. To consider the teacher's perspective, to put themselves in the position of the teacher and think about how an action would be perceived by him/her. "If I were the teacher, how would I feel about this?"
7. To remember their child's needs cannot overwhelm the needs of a class;
8. To look for the good in the teacher.
9. To accept the responsibility to help their child at home, supporting children's strengths and working on needs;
10. To inform educators of changing situations in the home which may have influenced learning;
11. To meet/talk with teachers at convenient, appropriate times (e.g., not interrupting a lesson in class);
12. To provide good role models for children.

Role of Children

Botrie and Wenger stated the roles of children as follows:

1. To become self-directed learners who take responsibility for their own learning.
2. To treat teachers and parents with respect because they are prime advocates and nurturers.
3. To seek help from both parents and teachers if required.

Botrie and Wenger further stated, "Wouldn't it be great in a school setting if all principals had a shared vision with their parents, teachers, and staff to be used as a model for student success?"

Two Processes for Developing a Shared Vision:

1. Each staff might work during a one-or two-day in-service to:

- Collaboratively discuss the school's beliefs about learning. First, teachers write their individual beliefs before sharing them with a partner. Finally, the group shares them as a whole, and forms a common list of beliefs.
- Identify what the school is doing to support these guiding principles of learning. This facilitates positive feelings about present programming, and helps other teachers become informed.
- Identify the practices that promote the successful implementation of these principles of learning in the school.
- Problem-solve ways of affecting change.
- Identify what the school is doing that does not support these beliefs. Discuss these practices to determine if they should be terminated.
- Include parents in these discussions.

2. Some staffs may find the following process more valuable:

- During grade level meetings explore, articulate, and reflect together on classroom practices.

- Consider and discuss the two questions given below.

    a. What do you do to support listening, reading, writing, and so on in your second or sixth grade classrooms?

    b. How do your programs support the continuum of learning throughout the school?

From this pragmatic, practical approach, teachers' beliefs will emerge. A small group forum creates a comfortable learning/sharing climate that promotes tolerance and acceptance of varying teaching philosophies.

If a parent/teacher handbook is a result of either process, invite a few parents to read the final draft. Parents can identify and clarify the teacher jargon that may confuse others. Including parents at this stage also offers them an opportunity to shape the final product. It says, "We value your involvement?"

Reinforcing and Extending Your School's Belief

- Plan school directions to facilitate implementation and understanding of guiding principles and supporting practices, for example, parent and teacher workshops.
- Publicize the principles of the school for parents, teachers, and students.
- Include them on the parents' bulletin board, in a newsletter, or refer to them when welcoming new parents or addressing parent groups.
- Teachers can refer to a classroom setting to guide their planning, teaching, practice, and evaluation.
- Help students become aware of the principles so that they better understand the thinking behind teachers' decisions on programming, grouping, evaluation, and so on.
- Visitors, such as occasional staff and student teachers, assimilate more easily if they understand the school's focus and beliefs.

- Post the vision statement throughout the school, in every classroom, and on newsletters to parents and correspondence.

Each school's beliefs about learning may be different, reflecting the needs of the community, students, and particular strengths or individual schools. Uniqueness of schools, when articulated to parents, helps them decide if a school best suits the needs of their child and their family.

We should be aware that informed parents who join a school community will be more supportive in the long run. The parent/school partnership becomes a win/win situation rather than a tug of war where each party tries to convince the other of the merit of their viewpoint(s).

The Parent Involvement Committee

The beliefs of a school can help determine its committee structure. Teachers can decide what areas to focus on to continue growth and establish appropriate committees. If a school believes that parental support is crucial component for student success, a small parent involvement committee might think about ways to include parents in the school. The establishment of such a committee legitimizes this issue and helps raise teacher consciousness about relationships with parents. When committees report back to the whole group, other teachers begin to consider parent/teacher issues more consciously.

Each school will determine its own methods of strengthening ties with parents. The ways to involve parents will be as creative as the staff involved in the planning. Teachers will gradually take ownership as they are asked to consider the problem and generate creative solutions. The most effective ways of dealing with each parent group will become evident as ideas are created, implemented, and assessed.

It would be helpful if schools created Parent Involvement Committees, as they help shape their relationship with parents.

Educators are less likely to present a knee-jerk reaction to a disgruntled parent, and will become aware of the parents' needs and the perspective of the school system. Schools, by establishing the committee, appear to place value on parents' voices. This perception helps strengthen parent/school relationships.

Parent Involvement Committees might generate discussion around one or two of the following questions throughout the year. Parent inclusion recognizes that schools need their involvement to create policies to establish parental support, ownership, commitment, knowledge and understanding.

Parents and Teachers: Joint Partners in School Policy?

Consider the following questions. It might be helpful to jot down your thoughts. The resultant responses will give you an overview of parent/teacher relationships in your school.

- How do we address the needs of working parents? Non-custodial parents? ESL (English as a Second Language) parents?
- How do we involve parents in developing our initiatives and our school focus (e.g. school values policy)?
- How do we explain our evaluation criteria to parents?
- How can we help parents network with one another?
- How can we draw parents, in a meaningful way, into the school?
- How can parents help support the beliefs of the school?
- How are parents involved when the school is developing and/or implementing an initiative?
- How do we welcome new families to our school?
- How are parents informed of weekly and monthly school events?
- What are the unique needs of the community we serve?
- How can parents be guided to support their children's academic and social success (e.g., homework, values)?
- Is there a consistency in reporting to parents?

- Does our reporting system need to be reassessed?
- How can the value of our policies be enhanced for parents (e.g., getting parent and staff input)?
- What directions should parent in-service take to best meet the needs of parents?
- How would our school look to a new parent?
- What process is employed when parents have an issue with a teacher?
- Does the staff understand how to diffuse conflict with a parent?
- What process is in place to handle parental concerns and questions about the school?
- How can we improve parent attendance at school events?
- How can schools use strong, informed parents to support the needs of families "at risk" (e.g., parents of children with learning disabilities)?
- How can parents support and encourage school spirit?
- How are parents informed of board wide issues (e.g., anti-racist policy, harassment and drug policies)?
- How can we assist parents to develop new knowledge re: basic home-related issues such as providing adult computer courses, child management courses and so on? (Botrie/ Wenger, pp. 13-20).

Quality parenting can save our children. Parents, this is so important. If someone asked you to name your biggest responsibility in life, you should say, "being a parent." Parents know their most important and most challenging job is rearing happy, successful children. Doing this takes time… lots of time. But today's busy lifestyles make finding time difficult. Many studies show parents spend only minutes a day with their children, and that's not enough. To reach their full potential in school and in life, kids need frequent, meaningful, undivided attention from parents or a positive adult figure in the home. The results can be incredible:

- Higher grades
- Better behavior

- Stronger language skills
- Improved relationships
- Positive self-image
- Pride and confidence

The earlier you start spending "quality" and "quantity" time with your child, the better off your child will become in life. But it is never too late. By making the most of each minute, you will create rewards that last a lifetime. It doesn't matter what your financial situation is. It doesn't matter what your living situation is. It doesn't matter if you are formally educated or not. It doesn't matter if you are single or married, rich or poor, young or old. Parents are still the most important person to the child.

You still can be a productive and caring parent. Expect children to develop good habits. Be repetitious. Try the 21-day concept. Experts have discovered that if you repeat an action every day for 21 days, it is likely to become automatic. So, parents for the next 21 days, expect your children to act on their new habits. After that, they'll find they do it without thinking about it. I am often reminded about a conversation I had with my late uncle Percy when he mentioned to me that his youngest son Kelvin was only interested in playing basketball. I replied to my uncle "What did you expect when you converted the backyard into a basketball court with spotlights around the house." Just as Kelvin practiced basketball for 21 days, if he practiced reading and doing his homework for 21 days, studying and learning would become automatic.

I am the oldest of 27 sisters and brothers; 16 sisters and 11 brothers. My mother and father weren't married. My mother and stepfather who raised me knew the importance of parenting and getting a good education. My mother only completed the third grade. Because your children know and trust you when you spend time with them, they will look up to you as role models. Children's habits, values, likes, and dislikes are most influenced by their parents, grandparents or a concerned and trusted relative. My mother would take me to church and school. We were required to say a blessing at the table before each meal. We ate together as a family even though we didn't have much to eat. My mother, grandmother, grandfathers, neighbors, relatives and teachers all helped to raise me. I was fortunate to have many parents to influence me. The same is true for children's interests, religious faith, attitudes about learning, and attitudes about other people, and even the words they learn. Parents have the most influence on all of these things. So, save our children, save our schools, because our children are our greatest resource. Children are our future and they are an extension of their parents. Our children know us and trust us when we spend time with them, they look up to us as role models.

The qualities that will determine how successful children will be in school and in life are influenced most by their parents. Parents' challenge is to find ways to spend time and lots of undivided attention, with their children. Then they need to be the best influence they can be on children during the time they spend with them. As a parent myself, I have four children, two girls and two boys and with plenty of praying, discipline, guidance and hard work they all are college graduates and currently married and employed.

Making the time usually involves sacrifices and tough choices; but it's worth it. The time parents spend with their children now will pay big dividends for the rest of their lives and the parent's lives. It's hard to say that about anything else parents might choose to do with their time. So, parents, take the time to make the time. Have fun, one-on-one with your children, and find time for family. Spend time learning together. Learn to talk and listen well. Be nosey and know what your children are doing and who their friends are. Have rules for your children and give them guidance. Always tell your children you love them and show them that you do. Time is one of the most valuable gifts you can give your child. Every minute you spend together is an investment that will pay off for life. So, parents invest in your children because you are preparing for their future.

As a child, I can remember attending three elementary schools in the same year and moving three times. We lived in a "shot gun" house; rent was $11.75 per week. I chopped and picked cotton for $3.00 a day and we moved when the rent was due, always at midnight. We never thought we were poor because my mother and stepfather always encouraged us to stay focused, study hard, stay in school, and they showered us with plenty of love and guidance. As a result of the quality time in my educational pursuits, my parents, grandparents, relatives, neighbors, and teachers spent with me, I acquired my doctorate degree at the age of 28.

Parents, be reminded that knowledge is power. No one can take this away from you. Learn everything that you can to be able to pass this knowledge on to your children. If your children can read, write, and compute with clarity and understanding and can articulate the issues, they will be successful in this competitive world. If not, they will find themselves even further behind in society.

Parents always do what you think is right for your children and whatever you do, do it on a consistent basis. Children respond to consistency and they grow to expect it, want it, appreciate it, and respect it. So parents, continue to fight for what's right for your children. Continue to be a positive role model for your children. Continue to challenge them and to challenge yourself, because our children are being raised at a time where positive role models are rare, where most of our children view being successful through material things.

Believe it or not, your six-year old won't wear the sneakers you bought him. Everyone, he says, is wearing shoes that cost $125 a pair-"Air Jordan's". Your ten-year old daughter wants to pierce her ears and other parts of her body. "Everyone else already has," she says. Parents, your teenager wants to go to a party where you think alcohol will be present. If she stays home, she says she will lose all her friends. Peer influence begins when children are young and increases, as they grow older. It is natural and healthy for children to rely more on friends as they mature. Sometimes peer pressure can be harmless. But, it can also cause kids to do poorly in school, to experiment with drugs or alcohol or to become sexually active.

Listed below are ten things I recommend parents do with their children on a consistent basis:

1. Listen to your child (because they too need to be heard and respected).
2. Help your child develop self-confidence (to be able to think for themselves).
3. Encourage your child to take part in positive activities.
4. Encourage your child to suggest other things to do (this makes them flexible and creative).
5. Get to know your child's friends (you need to know the company they are keeping).
6. Teach your child to foresee situations that may lead to trouble (this helps them to think and to know the difference between right and wrong).
7. Develop backup plans when your child is in a difficult situation she/he can't handle (this helps to develop alternative plans).
8. Teach your child how to say "no" to drugs, sex, crime, strangers, and other harmful things (this teaches values and respect).
9. Turn peer pressure into positive pressure (children should look for decent friends to do positive things with while they are growing up).
10. Talk with other parents at every opportunity (to compare successes and failures).

I know we can remember when we were in elementary, middle or high school. We all remember a teacher, good or bad. I can remember my sixth-grade teacher, Mr. Theodore Johnson, telling me if I got into a fight during the lunch period on the playground, he would take me into the "cloakroom" and whip me. Afterwards, Mr. Johnson took me to Mr. Bland's office, the principal, and he gave me my second whipping. Both of them repeatedly told me they were whipping me because they loved me, and they knew I could do better in school. Then the two of them took me home where my mother and stepfather gave me my third and fourth whippings. So, I decided that I couldn't sustain four whippings a day and survive.

As a result of all the discipline and attention I received as a child in school and at home, I looked forwarded to going to school everyday. Today, this would be called corporal punishment and truly not the most effective way to discipline children, but in the 1950's and 1960's, it worked well for me as a child growing up.

Today parents are raising children in a totally different environment than we did 40-50 years ago. The vast majority of parents today are younger, less formerly educated, and unmarried. Therefore, a parent's approach to rearing children and managing anger and discipline should require a great deal of patience, understanding, tolerance, caring, parenting skills, love and compassion. Therefore, the author suggests 10 ways parents can assist their child/children with managing anger. They are listed as follows:

1. Explain that anger is normal. It is how we manage it that counts.
2. Help your child identify signs of anger, from obvious (yelling or screaming) to subtle (an upset tummy or a headache).
3. Show understanding. You might say, "I can see that you're angry because I won't let you play until your homework's done."
4. Teach proven "cool-down" techniques. These include: counting to 10 or 20, or 100; taking 10 slow, deep breaths; writing the angry thought on paper, then tearing up the paper.
5. Have your child write a list of ways to handle anger better next time. Play-acting can help, too.
6. Encourage your child to talk about feelings in order to find the root of the anger.
7. Keep your child healthy, with enough rest and nutritious food.
8. Limit your child's viewing of violence in video games, movies, TV, and media in general.

9. Help your child handle stress. Some stress reducers are: listening to soothing music, exercising, and playing with a favorite pet.
10. Remind your child to respect the rights and feelings of others.

REMEMBER-PARENTS,

- Be a good role model
- Never use any kind of physical force on your child.

According to Dr. James Dobson, (Dare To Discipline, Wheaton, Il: Tyndale, 1987 and Dr. Teresa Langston, Parenting Without Pressure, A Parent's Guide. Colorado Springs, Co: NAV Press, 1993), effective discipline starts with understanding the important difference between "discipline and punishment." Discipline comes from the root word "disciple" and it means "to teach." It's an approach that focuses on teaching children appropriate behavior. On the other hand, punishment means "to chastise or correct." It negatively addresses misbehavior after it has occurred. Parents who often confuse these two concepts apply a lot of punishment with little or no discipline.

The key factor is simply this: the better you are with the discipline, the less you have to punish. Therefore, as parents you want to see yourselves as teachers.

Your goal should be to teach your children all they need to know that will enable them to function well as adults; things such as the important concepts between their behavior and its consequences (both good and bad), the concepts of accountability, responsibility, and appropriate ways to solve problems and make good choices.

Moreover, effective discipline always starts with positive parenting. Listed below are tips for positive parenting:

TIPS FOR POSITIVE PARENTING

Define boundaries (rules) before enforcing them. The child should know what is expected before being held responsible for it. (Parenting Without Pressure by Teresa Langston suggests "Arbitration" as an excellent time for this.) Remember, If you haven't defined or explained it, don't enforce it!

Respond with confident decisiveness when challenged. Always respond; never react. Nothing is more destructive to parental leadership than for a parent to disintegrate during a struggle. Therefore, give up the struggle without giving up the authority by offering choices.

1. Acknowledge the child's feelings.
2. Provide a choice or alternative.
3. Disengage from the behavior.

For example: "Sam, please set the table for dinner. Sam, I can see your frustration, but you have a choice here. You can choose to set the table or you can choose to loose tonight's television privileges. Sam, I am going to count to three and if you have not started setting the table, I will know what your choice is."

Distinguish between willful defiance and childish irresponsibility. Parental disciplinary response should be determined by the child's intention. Remember this when establishing consequences.

Willful defiance is a deliberate act of disobedience. It occurs when the child knows what his/her parents expect and is determined to do the opposite.

Childish irresponsibility results from a child being a child. Being forgetful, having accidents, short attention span, a low tolerance for frustration and the child is immature.

Reassure and teach after the confrontation is over. Children should be assured of parental love regardless of their behavior. The debriefing technique provides an excellent teaching opportunity. This technique simply asks the questions:

1. Why did you lose such and such?
2. What will happen if such and such happens again?
3. How can you do it differently in the future?

Avoid impossible demands. Be absolutely sure that your child is capable of delivering what you require.

Let love be your guide! A relationship that is characterized by genuine love and affection is likely to be a healthy one, even though some parental mistakes and errors are inevitable.

I think, in order to be a successful parent, not only would you have to be an effective disciplinarian, you must also be a good communicator as well. Dr. Teresa Langston states in her book, Parenting Without Pressure, A Parent's Guide, that when asked, most parents will say they want good communication with their children yet without realizing it, they're often the greatest roadblocks. We live with excessive stress in a fast-paced world that takes a tremendous toll on our bodies. Sadly, children can end up on the receiving end of chronic insensitive comments, and emotional unavailability.

Compounding this problem is the children's immaturity. Parents can lose sight of the fact that a twelve year old, 186-pound boy is as close to age ten as he is to age fifteen and will act like a twelve year old about half of the time. Teenagers are especially notorious for responding to parental dialog by acting bored, flip, silly, coy, or hearing-impaired. This can cause parents to react with verbal bashing that can emotionally cripple kids. Emotional walls are built with bricks of thoughtless words. This is another way to destroy relationships, so longed for, and ensure they never materialize.

Avoid communication pitfalls with this list of suggestions:

TIPS FOR GOOD COMMUNICATION

Always treat children with courtesy, kindness and respect. Good communication flows from mutual respect and understanding among family members. When children are treated with the same courtesy, kindness, and respect the parents give their best friends, it sends a strong message of love and support. Effective communication is generous with comments like, "please" and "thank you." Make requests instead of giving orders, and always be quick to say, "I am sorry" when you are wrong.

Listen actively by repeating your child's feelings with empathy and understanding. Simple acknowledgement of the child's feelings will always get you a lot of mileage. Not only do you validate the child but you also put the child in a position to then hear what you have to say. Remember, agreement isn't necessary in order to describe your child's feeling. You simply put yourself in your child's shoes. For example, your daughter is up-set because her best friend is moving out of state. Avoid saying, "you will have another best friend." Instead reply with, "You sound pretty sad about your best friend moving."

Avoid misunderstandings with reflective listening. To help your child feel understood and to avoid misunderstandings, acknowledge the meaning of what the child has said. Simply rephrase the message. For example, your son states his desire for a part-time job claiming that he can handle it. Your response is, "It seems to me that you have figured out how to keep your grades up, maintain your existing commitments and add a job to your existing busy schedule."

Cool off before you talk, and choose your words carefully. Children really do believe what a parent tells them and they will always reach up or stoop down to parental expectations. Therefore, make sure that what you say is positive and builds up rather than tears down. Also helpful, avoid comments that start with "Why" followed by "can't you," "don't you," and "won't you." Consider rephrasing words such as hyperactive, strong-willed and daydreamer with energetic, tenacious and creative.

Remember, if you want to be heard, you first must be available and listen. Take the time to make yourself available. Only when a child genuinely feels heard and understood does a parent have a prayer that the child will listen.

Make yourself available even at inconvenient times and places. Create an atmosphere that is safe for kids to explore their thoughts and feelings even if you don't agree. Also, be careful about supplying solutions. Rarely do kids want solutions; what they want is a listening ear.

Listen more and talk less. Listening is not the same as hearing. It goes beyond the words and gets to the heart of what is being said while acknowledging its importance. Listen to body language as well as words. Remember, talking is sharing but listening is caring.

While listening, don't mentally rehearse your reply. Don't mentally rehearse your reply while your child is speaking. Instead, listen to what is being said.

Use plenty of "I" messages. "I" messages take the blame out of communication. The format sounds like this: when you …., I feel…, and I wish….,
1. Describe the behavior.
2. State your feeling.
3. State the consequence how you'd like it to be.

For example, "When you don't complete your chores, I feel overwhelmed because it adds to my list of things I need to complete."

Hold Weekly Family Meetings. Weekly family meetings provide all family members with a platform to be heard and understood. They also create a format for families to formulate rules, determine operational boundaries and deal with problem areas while they are small. Suggestions for family meetings:

1. Meet at a regularly scheduled time each week, not just when there is a crisis.
2. Establish a time limit. Thirty minutes is long enough for most families.
3. Give everyone an opportunity to be heard.
4. If needed, use an agenda to stay on track.
5. Use tackling difficult issues as an opportunity to teach problem solving.
6. Discuss good things happening in the family.
7. Plan for family fun and outings.
8. To ensure participation, only pay allowance and provide lunch money at the conclusion of your family meeting.
9. Read together as a family.

Sources: Dr. James Dobson, Dare to Discipline, Wheaton, Ill. Tyndale House Publishers, 1987 and Dr. Teresa Langston, Parenting Without Pressure, A Parent's Guide, Colorado Springs, Colorado. NAV Press, 1993. "http://www.parentingwithoutpressure"

All communications with children are crucial, verbal or non-verbal. Since non-verbal communication is sometimes difficult for children to follow and understand, parents must make sure they are using good non-verbal communication. Non-verbal body language is a strong form of communication. A vast majority of communication is in the tone of voice and a small percent is in content. So, parents, always check your body language and the tone of your voice when communicating with your children. Make sure both are positive. Positive body language includes providing focused attention, having a pleasant facial expression, and sometimes leaning forward in your chair in order to make eye contact with your children.

Parents, I challenge you to try to recite and be committed to these words everyday of your child's youth and you will see great results in your child's growth and development: "*I will persist, until I succeed, I will persist, until I succeed. As long as I have breath in me, I will persist. If I persist long enough, I will win, but I must also be willing to persist in helping my child/children to succeed in life."*

Parents as Models

While speaking at a parental involvement conference in Orlando, Florida, February, 2003, I asked a group of parents to describe a good parent. Their answers pointed out some of the ways that parents do make a difference. None of the answers involved providing material things. They came from caring parents who spent quality time with their children. The following list which reflects the parent's ideas of the qualities of good parenting comes from the book "Parent and Children Together: Parents as Models" published by The Family Literacy Center, in Bloomington, IN.:

1. Soften discipline with kindness.
2. Laugh at knock-knock jokes (even the zillionth time).
3. Tell their kids they love them, A lot!.
4. Know that children can't be perfect.
5. Celebrate special moments, no matter how small.
6. Can smile after only a few hours of sleep.
7. Put love notes in lunch boxes.
8. Accept that a child may not turn out exactly as you prefer or want them to be.
9. Be there when needed, out of the way when not—and able to recognize the difference.

Children benefit greatly when parents take an active role in their education. Children will usually:
1. Enjoy learning and school life more.
2. Develop confidence in themselves.
3. Improve their skills and attitudes and do better in school.
4. Be better prepared for the future.

From the very beginning of their lives, children imitate others. They imitate much of what they see and hear. Most parents are unaware of their role as prime models. But when parents "show" how much they love and care for their children, children can only benefit in positive ways because they will imitate that love and care.

We are also models for our children when we face problems. Consider the following situation: A mother finds her preschool daughter angrily taking a book from another child and then sees her slap the other child's arm. The mother furiously jerks her daughter by the arm and starts shaking her, yelling, "I'll teach you to play rough!" This mother is unknowingly modeling the very behavior that she wants to discourage in her daughter.

How could the mother have handled this situation differently? She could have stepped in and said, "I know you want her book, honey, but you must not hurt your friend. Give the book back to her and tell her you are sorry for hurting her. Ask her if you can borrow it after she has finished with it. Then I will help you find something to do while you're waiting for your turn." This approach makes it clear that hurtful behavior is not allowed, and it also gives the child a positive way to deal with her need. Most importantly, it shows the child that she can rely on her mother for advice when she needs it. Our children need to know that they can trust us for help, and for love. Remember, to be a model means to create an image of behavior in the minds of our children.

Even though parents may not be teachers, parents can do a lot to help their children succeed in school. Here are some ways that parents can create images in their child's mind that will help with school:

1. **READ:** Take time to read. When you read books, magazines, and newspapers, you show your child that reading is valuable. Important adults like Mom, Dad or significant family members should do it all the time.

2. **WRITE:** Write notes to your child. Have your child help write grocery lists. Let your child see you write a letter to a

friend or to your parents. Then ask your child to enclose a note of her own.

3. **SHOW INTEREST**: When you show interest in your children's schoolwork they sense that you care and that you want them to do well. It only takes a minute at a meal to ask what interesting or important things happened today in school, and then a few minutes to listen to the answers.

4. **SHOW CURIOSITY:** Show your curiosity by asking your child to teach you something she/he learned that day. Also, develop an interest in learning something new yourself. Everyone is a learner—that's the image you want to leave with your child.

5. **SHOW PATIENCE:** Keep calm and be helpful when things don't go well, for example, when your son doesn't think he will be able to get his report done on time or screams, "I hate math!" when he can't figure out a problem. Sit down with him and say "Maybe we'll be able to work it out."

The point of these examples is to remind parents of the many opportunities they have to act as a model for learning and literacy. These small actions on parents' part make it more likely that their children will do well in school. As parents become more aware of how they influence their children, they can examine ways of changing their behavior so that it is more in line with the beliefs and values that parents want to pass on to their children.

Of course, no one can be a perfect model all the time, and often parents act in ways that they would rather not have their children imitate. The way parents choose to respond to their imperfections, however, provides an example for their children. It is worth admitting to children the mistakes parents make.

There certainly are no surefire answers that will produce predictable results when it comes to rearing children. As parents, you make decisions each day based on specific situations, on what you already know about your children, and on what you desire your relationships with them to be like. By realizing that you are models for your children, you can adopt a more deliberate attitude in shaping what your children learn.

Questions about Parenting

Most parents have questions concerning their children's behavior. I would like to answer a few questions and offer some suggestions to help you be a good model for your children. A young mother made the following statement:

Question: I realize now as a young, single parent that school and learning are much more important than I realized when I was growing up. I want my children to get a good education. How can I help my children value school and learning?

Answer: The high school dropout rate is proof that many kids do not see the value of school. Most children are not likely to fall for the old line, I want you to do better than I did". You want the best for your children, of course. Probably the best thing you can do as a parent is to get involved in learning yourself. That's your best strategy for convincing your children to keep learning.

Question: My children aren't learning anything at that school. I don't like the teachers. They have nasty attitudes. I didn't learn anything when I went to that school. Are the teachers doing the same things to my children that they did to me?

Answer: As a parent you have to break this cycle of negative thoughts about the school. Be extremely careful about criticizing the school and teachers around your children. Get your attitude together first. Try to be tolerant and forgiving. Get involved with the school. Parents can volunteer time, join the PTA/PTO, or school advisory council/board. Talk with the teachers and principals calmly, with an open-mind and with some ideas of how you might help correct/ improve situations you find unsatisfactory.

Question: My child repeats everything I say to other children and other adults. How can I stop this behavior?

Answer: Be careful what you say around your children especially something not worth repeating. Most certainly children will repeat what they hear and at the most inappropriate time. The rule of thumb is: if you don't want to hear it again, don't say it. Children are innocent and they are always listening and learning. They learn from parents, grandparents, other close adults and older children.

PARENTS: Consider
- A child's brain develops most rapidly from birth to 4 years old.
- 50% of a child's intelligence is acquired by age 4; 80% by age 8.
- By age 5 your child's personality, self concept, emotional development and character will be almost complete.

Old sayings are especially applicable to children.
- An ounce of prevention is worth a pound of cure.
- A stitch in time saves nine.

A small investment now can prevent learning and emotional problems later. In order to read, a child must be in a comfortable, supportive, noncompetitive environment whether at home or school. To help make the child to be more comfortable, parents need to introduce their children to new things, people and situations. You are a model! Your child will imitate your behavior, good or bad! Reading everyday to your child will help in many ways. Your child needs love… but this does not mean doing as the child pleases. Your child is an individual. Do not compare him/her with others. Your child needs repetition in order to learn. Many children understand 20,000 to 40,000 words in first grade.

The role of the parent in education is critical because the home environment is vital to children's educational achievement. Not even the best school can do the job alone. Parents can, and should, take advantage of opportunities at home to teach their children in an informal way. Teaching academics and developing strong, one-on-one relationships with children are effective ways to develop self-esteem and interpersonal relationship skills. As children continue in school, all parents, uncles, aunts, cousins, grandparents, and all adults in children's lives, need to remember that they are vital partners with teachers in the education of their children. (pp 2-10).

PARENT INVOLVEMENT IN THE READING PROGRAM

Parents, love of reading is one of the greatest gifts that home and school can give children. This love is usually not taught but caught. Learning to read is a long, continuous and complicated process that involves a child's mind, heart, body, and feeling. Because reading is so very important, it is a task to be undertaken by home and school together.

Reading builds upon previous experiences and language skills that children have. Parents can do much to enhance skills here that will make a significant contribution to the child's eventual reading achievement. Listed below are specific things that you are encouraged to do:

1. Listen to children; give them many opportunities to use language; don't become impatient if they cannot express themselves clearly.

2. Take time to explain things that are happening to and around children. When you ask them to do something, tell them why it should be done.

3. Point out parts of the environment that children might miss. Give labels to these things ie…lakes, rivers, forests, mountains, and roads, etc.

4. Introduce new experiences. Take trips, provide the opportunity to join clubs and other organizations. These things will help to foster new interests.

5. Point out letters and words as they are encountered in the child's everyday world or on television: ex., stop, restaurant, and titles on movie marquees. Do this in as natural a way as possible and don't become upset if the child doesn't seem interested or remember the words.

6. Children usually model themselves after their parents; therefore parents should provide a good reading model by reading themselves.

7. Read to children. This is an excellent way to build the language foundation and thinking skills necessary for becoming an effective reader. Choose books carefully for reading to them.

8. Encourage your children to secure their own library card, and take them to the public library. Take advantage of the special children's program set up by your public library.

9. Buy books if they express an interest in them.

10. Let your child have a special place to keep his books-even if it is one shelf of your bookshelf. Encourage him to fill his shelf with books of his choice.

11. If your child is developing new interests, try to find reading materials that fit these interest areas.

12. Subscribe to a children's book club or magazine. If you are unsure of choosing the correct books for your child, these publications suggest books of specific grade and age levels.

13. Read textbooks from science or social studies to children in order to help deal with the facts and concepts introduced in class.

14. Be sure your child is up to par physically. Learning to read demands the best of his/her effort, concentration and clear thinking. Have your child examined regularly and be sure his/her hearing and vision are normal.

15. Spend time REALLY talking with and listening to your child.

One of our leading authorities on parental involvement, Dr. Grace O'Connor writes in her book titled <u>"Helping Your Children: A Basic Guide for Parents,"</u> (1966) the following: Parents together are a child's security. Parents are the people a child wants to copy. Parents are the people a child wants to please. Do your best to be good parents. You want to be proud of your children. Your children want to be proud of you. You will make mistakes. Everyone makes mistakes. Don't worry about the mistakes. But try to do better next time.

Remember:
- ❖ If you want an honest child, be an honest parent.
- ❖ If you want a kind and fair child, be a kind and fair parent.
- ❖ If you want a friendly child, be a friendly parent
- ❖ If you want a clean child, be a clean parent
- ❖ If you want a happy loving child, be a happy loving parent.

Who Cares?
- ❖ There are times when we wonder-
- ❖ Who cares about me? Who cares about my problems?
- ❖ Who cares that my children need help?
- ❖ Who cares that my husband needs work?
- ❖ Who cares what happens to me?
- ❖ Who cares what happens to my family?

Your place of worship cares. Your minister will listen and help. Your priest or rabbi will listen and help. There are groups such as the Boy's Club/Girl's Club of America, YMCA and the YWCA. There are athletic groups at the "Y's" in your town. The "Y's" have social groups for all ages.

Your city cares. That is why they have social agencies and public health departments. That is why they have good schools. That is why they have adult education classes. That is why they have a free public library for you.

People do care. We need never be afraid or lonely. We may need to look for help. But it is there for the asking <u>(Helping Your</u>

<u>Children: A Basic Guide for Parents,</u> O'Connor pp100-101). So, parents, always be proactive in taking the initiative to do your best in rearing your children. Being a parent today is hard work, but there are great, great, rewards.

Chapter 3

The Role of Family in Rearing Children

"Knowing ones family history gives you a sense of direction, a sense of belonging, hope and pride."

There is an old African proverb that says, *"It takes an entire village to raise a child."* Therefore, it takes many committed adult figures to have a positive impact on children's lives, which is why the role of the family is important. For the purpose of this guidebook, family is defined as any responsible and concerned adult or adults related to the child or children by blood or marriage. These significant others must be interested in the growth, development and safety of the child or children. This could be a grandparent, uncle, aunt, cousin, niece, nephew, sister or brother. In addition, other adults may be considered like family, i.e., godparents, athletic coaches, teachers, and family friends. Therefore, the terms parent (s) and extended family members would include the above references as they relate to the definition of family in this book.

According to the book titled, "The Secret of Family Happiness", *Watch Tower Bible and Tract Society of Pennsylvania & New York, 1996,* the family is the oldest institution on earth, and it plays a vital role in human society. Throughout history, strong families have helped to make strong societies. The family is the best arrangement for bringing up children to be mature adults.

A happy family is a haven of safety and security. Envision the ideal family for a moment. During their evening meal, caring parents or extended members sit with their children and discuss the events of the day. Children chatter excitedly as they tell their father, mother, grandparents, uncles, aunts, cousins, or any other trusting responsible adult about what happened at school. The relaxing time spent together refreshes everyone for another day in the world outside.

In a happy family, a child knows that his/her father, mother or extended family member will provide the needed care when he/she gets sick, perhaps taking turns at the bedside through the night. The child knows that he/she can go to his/her father, mother or extended family members with the problems of his/her young life and get advice and support. Yes, the child feels safe, no matter how trouble-filled the outside world may be.

When children grow up, they usually get married and have a family of their own. "A person realizes how indebted he/she is to his/her parents or extended family members when they have children of their own," says an oriental proverb. With a deep sense of gratitude and love, the grown children try to make their own families happy, and they also care for their now aging parents, who delight in company of the grandchildren.

Perhaps at this point you are thinking: well, I love my family, but it is not like the one just described. My spouse and I work different schedules and hardly see each other. We talk mostly about money problems. Or do you say, "My children and grandchildren live in another town, and I never get to see them?" Yes, for reasons often beyond the control of those involved, much family life is less than ideal. Still, some lead happy family lives. How? Is there a secret of family happiness? The answer is yes. But before discussing what it is, we should answer an important question (Watch Tower Bible and Tract Society, 1996).

What Is A Family?

In the Western part of the world, most families consist of a father, mother, and children. Grandparents may live in their own households as long as they can. While contact is kept up with more distant relatives, duties toward these are limited. However, other families have become increasingly common in recent years such as the single-parent family, the step-family, and the family whose parents are not living together for one reason or another.

Common in some cultures is the extended family. In this arrangement, if possible, grandparents are routinely looked after by their children, and close ties and responsibilities extend to distant relatives. For instance, family members may help to support, raise, and even pay for the education of their nieces, and nephews, or more-distant relatives. The principles to be discussed in this book apply also to extended families.

According to Dr. Teresa Langston in her book, <u>Parenting Without Pressure: A Parenting Guide Book</u> she stated, "I will never forget the sorrow in the voice of a mom as she told a group of parents that because of her divorce, she and her boys were no longer going to be a family. She was certain that the reality of family life would gradually disappear. Unfortunately, for her the word family meant having a mom and a dad and 3.2 kids living under the same roof, with a van in the garage and a dog in the doghouse."

Many families no longer consist of the stereotypical husband, wife, three kids and a dog, all living under the same roof. Because of the increase in divorce and the growing number of children born to single parents, families today are defined simply as all of the people who live in the same household. Ideally, however, they are committed to one another; spend time together, and share values, beliefs, warm memories, and family traditions. This single mom and her children are very definitely a family, but the quality of life her family experiences depends largely on her.

Remember, parents, that this is not a dress rehearsal. What you do with your family doesn't include the possibility of giving a better performance later. The life you live today for you and your children is all there is. Be it good or bad, tomorrow it is history. Make it good for yourself and for your children.

The Role Parents Play in the Family in Rearing Children

As can be easily understood, the way parents react to these situations is of crucial importance. In dealing with their children, parents must see to it that each child is encouraged in some positive or cooperative direction which is independent of those taken by the other children in the family. Because of their own ambitions for their children, parents often fail to see the value of any activities which can be useful and satisfying to their children, but which do not fit their own particular standards. For example, parents with high academic aspirations for their children are often upset over the failure of a second child to repeat the academic prowess of the first. They do not understand that the second child is unwilling to compete in any area which is dominated by the first child. Therefore, his/her choice is in a different, often opposite, direction. Any attempt by the parent to push the second child in the direction of the first is almost inevitably met with great resistance. Why can't you be a good student like your sister/brother? Is the frequent lament of frustrated parents who put their own ambitions for a child ahead of his/her self interest? If the first child is academically inclined, it is the wise parent who encourages the second child in any useful activity he/she likes, whether it is mechanical, athletic, or social. Parents are often mystified to discover that when the first child has finished school and left home, the second child, who has been noticeably indifferent to his/her studies, all of a sudden becomes an academic wizard. Parents who understand the dynamics behind this behavior will see it as being purposive, though the child is not aware of the true nature of her/his goal.

The major danger facing parents if they are unwilling or unable to understand the inclinations of their children, is that one child may decide he cannot get recognition through positive competition with his brothers or sisters, but he can gain a great deal of attention by going in the opposite direction. He then becomes what is aptly termed "the best worst." If the child is lazy, irresponsible, disruptive, or does poor work at school, one can be sure that this will call down scolding, punishment, and admonition to do better, as well as parental despair, which is exactly what he/she wants. Every effort to make the child improve is met with more resistance. The tragedy is that often children train themselves in these habits to the degree that when the need for this kind of attention is gone, they have not learned to function in any other way.

The same characteristics develop in the various positions in deprived homes, but the ground rules are not the same. Because of their own discouragement in facing a hostile and indifferent world, parents are either unable or unwilling to provide any kind of encouragement for children who seek to be constructive. As a result, children are often left to fend for themselves, and only extreme behavior like fighting, vandalism, and destructiveness is enough to get the parents' attention. In school such a child feels lost; he/she sees no value in learning. She/he is usually confronted with a succession of failures from the minute he/she enters school, either drops out or "sits" out for a term. Violence, sex and drugs seem to be the only answer to this kind of discouragement.

Children are always learning. They learn from adults. They can communicate with you even before they can talk or walk by making different sounds and body gestures. Children have what I call a natural built in instinct to survive in life. They have a way of letting you know when they are wet or have soiled their diaper. For example, they let you know when they are hungry, sleepy, in pain or when they need to be held.

Parents, grandparents or family members have to be careful how they address these behavioral patterns during this early stage of a child's life. Because the child is constantly observing and monitoring how the parent(s), grandparent(s), or family member(s) are responding to their demands and out cries. This starts a chain reaction and a behavior pattern that will last the child for a lifetime. How you respond as parent(s), grandparent(s), or family member(s) are the differences between a child developing good or bad behavior or an attitude about life and how to get what he or she wants (Langston "http://www.parentingwithoutpressue.com").

After carefully observing my granddaughter, Lauren Bacall, during her visits with me, starting at three months, six months, twelve months, eighteen months, and twenty-four months, I witnessed first hand a tremendous growth in her personality and overall behavior. From three months on, Lauren Bacall started to respond to sounds and ways in which people reacted around her when she made certain gestures or demands. This is the time when parents, grandparents, and family members should begin to teach the child words by using pictures, hand gestures, discipline and manners. Be sure you do these activities on a consistent basis, because these are the most effective ways a child learns and retains what they were taught through repetition.

By two years old, my granddaughter is walking, talking, responding to her name and telling us what she wants and doesn't want. She enjoys watching her granddaddy wash dishes, shave, and water the lawn. As a result of her observing and monitoring my behavior, my granddaughter has developed a fascination to play in water. Parents, grandparents and family members, these are learned behaviors, because a child is a product of their environment, good or bad. This is where our parenting skills come into play and it pays off. None of the things I mentioned above require money, just simply a little of parents, grandparents or family members' time, love, attention and commitment.

In today's society, because generations of young parents are not rearing their children, the role of grandparents has changed from grandchildren making occasional visits to sole caregiver. In the state of Florida, over 260,000 grandparents are raising their grandchildren. More than 5,000,000 grandparents in the United States are raising grandchildren today. This demonstrates how effective the role of family is through grandparents. Grandparents have become the stabilizing force to the child or children in many homes throughout America.

THE POWER OF GRANDPARENTS

Children have a very special relationship with grandma and grandpa. That's why grandparents can be such powerful allies in helping keep a kid off drugs. Grandparents are cool and relaxed. They're not on the firing line every day. Some days a kid hates her/his folks. He/she never hates his/her grandparents. Grandparents ask direct, point-blank, embarrassing questions that parents are too nervous to ask:

- "Who's the girl?"
- "How come you're doing poorly in history?"
- "Why are your eyes always red?"
- "Did you go to the doctor? What did the doctor say?"

The same kid who cons his/her parents is ashamed to lie to grandparents. Without betraying their trust, a loving, understanding grandparent can discuss the danger of drugs openly with the child they adore, and should. Research provides the following information about children and drug use:

- The average age of first-time drug use among teens is 13. Some children start at 9.
- 1 out of 4 American children between the ages of 9 and 12 is offered illegal drugs by adults. 22% of these children receive the offer from a friend and 10% named a family member as their source.
- Illegal drugs can be linked to increased violence, poor performance in school, AIDS, birth defects, drug-related crimes, and homelessness.

As a grandparent, you hold a special place in the hearts and minds of your grandchildren. Share your knowledge, love, and faith in them. Use your power as an influencer to steer your grandchildren away from drugs. Grandma and grandpa, continue to talk to your grandkids. You don't realize the power and influence you have to save them. It is crucial for parents and grandparents to make a concerted effort to keep their children and grandchildren off drugs;

but, it is as equally important to provide a safe and positive living environment for them.

James Dobson also stated in his book, "MAKING HOME A POSITIVE PLACE" the following instructions:

"**Create a Safe Environment**: Make your home a safe place for all family members. In addition to not permitting physical confrontations, don't allow verbal mistreatment. Insist all family members treat one another with courtesy, kindness and respect.

Teach Constructive Conflict Resolution: There is not a problem in having a problem. However, there is a problem in not constructively dealing with it. Handle conflict through cooperation, negotiation, and problem solving. Family meetings provide an excellent format for brainstorming possible solutions to problems. On occasion, however, you can agree to disagree on strong issues. You don't have to agree on everything and you can still love each other.

Grab Every Opportunity to Spend Unstructured Time. It takes time to get to know a young person, to feel her/his hurts and understand his/her problems. Look for opportunities to spend time with your children. For example, play catch or shoot baskets, play video games or board games, build a snowman or sand castle, help with homework or daily chores, go for a walk, ride bikes, or simply read a story.

Plan Family Fun. Spending time together provides the opportunity to make happy memories from which the family can draw on during difficult times. These might include summer picnics, family story telling sessions, trips to the beach, backyard barbecues, or even learning a sport together as a family. Use arbitration as an opportunity to discuss and plan a monthly family time. Then make it a priority and put it on the calendar.

My grandfather was a prolific storyteller. Three nights a week, he would spend hours during the evenings telling family stories to his children and grandchildren. This gave me a sense of pride, a sense of family history, a sense of self worth and appreciation while having fun as a family and extended family.

Laugh Often. Mary G. Durkin, in <u>Making Your Family Work,</u> suggests that you can lighten your burden and make the task of parenting more rewarding if you learn to laugh. Durkin writes, *"When you trip, humor will soften the fall. You can then approach seemingly unsolvable family problems with the old cliché, 'If I don't laugh, I'll cry.'"* Additionally, Psychiatrist Christian Hageseth describes a sense of humor as a broad, optimistic perception of life, and suggests that it can ease tension and improve communication. By keeping your sense of humor and lightening up a little, you make family life much more positive and upbeat. It's important to remember, however, never confuse humor and ridicule. Laugh with your children, never at them. And teach all the family members that a good time should never be at the expense of one person for the family.

Teach Values. Families teach children societal rules and behavioral expectations. Additionally, from the family children learn morals, values, and attitudes. They also learn about relationships and what is considered important. Your actions and your words teach about love, honesty, courage, self-discipline, chastity, loyalty, fairness, empathy, tolerance, respect, and right from wrong.

Establish Family Traditions. Another way to make memories and have fun is through family traditions. Traditions simply celebrate the family, cultivate family identity, build hopefulness and cement family ties. They don't have to be elaborate affairs, just relevant to your family. Your family rituals or traditions might be the special way you celebrate the holidays, acknowledge a family member's milestone (such as a birthday) or honor a family member's achievement (such as a good report card). Celebrating family traditions through established and planned programs will have long lasting memories for the family. It brings a group of people together in an organized fashion to show honor, respect, and appreciation. This is a tradition that children can and will carry on throughout their lives and their children's, children's lives and generations to come. (Langston, http://www.parentingwithoutpressure.com).

The Family Under Stress. Today, the family is changing, sad to say, not for the better. An example is seen in India, where a wife may live with the family of her husband and work in the home under the direction of her in-laws. Now-a-days, though, it is not uncommon for Indian wives to seek employment outside the home, yet they are apparently still expected to fulfill their traditional roles in the home. The question raised in many lands is, compared with other members of the family, how much work should a woman with an outside job be expected to do in the home?

In Oriental societies, strong extended-family ties are traditional. However, under the influence of Western-style individualism and the stress of economic problems, the traditional extended family is weakening. Many, therefore, view care of aged family members as a burden rather than as a duty or a privilege. Some elderly parents are abused. Indeed, abuse and neglect of the aged are found in many countries today.

Divorce is becoming increasingly common. In Spain, the divorce rate increased to 1 out of 8 marriages by the beginning of the final decade of the 20th century, a big jump from 1 out of 100 just 25 years before. Britain, with reportedly the highest divorce rate in Europe (4 out of 10 marriages are expected to fail), has seen a surge in the number of single-parent families.

Many in Germany seem to be abandoning the traditional family altogether. The 1990's saw 35 percent of all German households made up of a single person and 31 percent made up of just two individuals. The French too are marrying less often, and those who do marry, divorce more often and earlier than used to be the case. Growing numbers prefer to live together without the responsibilities of marriage. Comparable trends are seen worldwide.

What about children? In the United States and many other lands, more and more are born out of wedlock, some to young teenagers. Many teenage girls have a number of children from different fathers. Reports from around the world tell of millions of homeless children roaming the streets. Many of these children are escaping from abusive homes or are cast out by families that can no longer support them.

Yes, the family is in crisis. In addition to what has already been mentioned, teenage rebellion, child abuse, spousal violence, alcoholism, and other devastating problems rob many families of happiness. For a great number of children and adults, the family is far from being a haven.

Why the family crisis? Some blame the present day family crisis on the entry of women into the workplace. Others point to today's moral breakdown and additional causes are also cited. Almost two thousand years ago, a well-known lawyer foretold that many pressures would afflict the family, when he wrote: "In the last days, critical times hard to deal with will be here. For men will be lovers of themselves, lovers of money, self-assuming, haughty, blasphemers, disobedient to parents, unthankful, disloyal, having no natural affection, not open to any agreement, slanderers, without self-control, fierce, without love of goodness, betrayers, headstrong, puffed up with pride, lovers of pleasures rather than lovers of human beings." In a world with conditions such as these, should there be any wonder why many families are in crisis?

Indeed, the joy of parenthood is a precious reward. However, those who have children soon realize that along with the joy, parenthood brings responsibilities. In many homes around the world, men view child training as chiefly woman's work. To whom should parents look for help in raising their children? What responsibility do fathers have in the raising of children?

Does your community expect a woman to give birth to as many children as possible? Rightfully, how many children a married couple has is their personal decision. What if parents lack the means to feed, clothe, and educate numerous children? Surely, the couple should consider this when deciding on the size of their family.

Some couples who cannot support all of their children entrust relatives with the responsibility to raise some of them. Is this practice desirable? Not really, and it does not relieve the parents of their obligation toward their children.

But babies need more. From the moment of birth, their brains are ready to receive and store information, and parents are the primary source of this. Take language as an example. Researchers say that how well a child learns to talk and to read is thought to be closely related to the nature of the child's early interaction with his/her parents. Talk and read to your child from birth on. Soon the child will want to copy you, and before long you will be teaching the child to read. Likely, the child will be able to read before entering school. That will be especially helpful if you live in a community where teachers are few and classrooms are crowded.

Yes, parents need to be examples, companions, communicators, and teachers. Ethical qualities must first be in the parent's heart. The parent must love the truth and live it. Only then can you reach the child's heart. Why? Because children are influenced more by what they see than by what they hear.

Be a companion, speak with your children often. This requires spending time with the children no matter how busy the parents are. Children are deserving of parent's time.

Be a communicator, spending time with your child will help you to communicate. The more you communicate, the better you will discern how his/her personality is developing. Remember, though, communicating is more than talking. "I had to develop the art of listening," said a mother in Brazil. "Listening with my heart," her patience bore fruit when her son began to share his feelings with her.

Children need "a time to laugh and a time to skip about," and a time for recreation. Recreation is very productive when parents and children enjoy it together. It is a sad fact that in many homes recreation means watching television. While some television programs may be entertaining, many destroy good values, and watching television tends to stifle communication in a family. Therefore, why not do something creative with your children? Sing, play games, associate with friends, and visit enjoyable places. Such activities encourage communication. Most parents know that getting information into a child's head is not easy. Many do not naturally hunger for academics. Parents need to find ways to develop that longing in their child.

By being an example, a companion, a communicator, and a teacher, you can help your child from his/her earliest years to form a close personal relationship with you. This relationship will encourage your child to be happy as a lark. He/she will strive to live up to the things you've instilled in her/him through the years when faced with peer pressure and temptations. Always, help your child to appreciate your precious relationship.

THE VITAL NEED OF DISCIPLINE

Discipline is training that corrects the mind and heart. Children need it constantly. Parents should discipline with love. Discipline based on love can be conveyed by reasoning. Hence, we are told to listen to discipline. How should discipline be given?

Effective Discipline: One meaningful form of discipline is to make children feel the unpleasant consequences of wrong behavior. If, for instance, your child makes a mess, cleaning it up without help may make the strongest impression. Has the child treated someone unfairly? Requiring an apology may correct this wrong trend. Another form of discipline is the denial of privileges for a time in order to drive home the needed lesson. In this way the child learns the wisdom of sticking to the right principles.

73

Protect Your Child From Harm: Many adults look back on their childhood as a happy time. They recall a warm feeling of safety, a certainty that their parents would look after them no matter what. Parents want their children to feel that way, but today's degenerated world, it is harder than it used to be to keep children safe.

Seek Guidance: Truly, the training of a child from infancy is a challenge, but believing parents do not have to face challenge alone. This is where the role of the family concept comes into play. Young people need the security of consistent discipline even if they do not always readily agree with the restrictions and rules. It is frustrating if rules are frequently changed, depending on the way a parent feels at the time. Further, if teenagers receive encouragement and help, as needed, in coping with differences, shyness, or lack of self-confidence, they will likely grow up to be more stable. Teenagers also appreciate it when they receive the trust that they have earned. Parents can be comforted to know that when peace, stability, and love exist within the household, the children usually flourish. Many youngsters have risen above even a bad home environment, coming from families marked by alcoholism, violence, or some other harmful influence, and have grown up to be fine adults. Hence, if you provide a home where your teenagers feel secure and know that they will receive love, affection, and attention, even if that support is accompanied by reasonable restriction and discipline, they are very likely to grow up to be adults of whom you are proud.

Protect Your Family From Destructive Influences: You are about to send your little one to school, and it is pouring rain. How do you handle the situation? Do you let her/him go skipping out the door without any rain gear? Or do you pile on so many layers of protective clothing that she/he can hardly move? Of course, you do neither. You give the child just what is needed to keep dry.

In a similar way, parents must find a balanced way to protect their family from the destructive influences that rain down on them from many sources -- the entertainment industry, the media, peers, and at times even the schools. Some parents do little or nothing to shield their family. Others, viewing nearly all outside influences as harmful, are so restrictive that the children feel as if they were suffocating. Is a balance possible?

As noted by many counselors and psychologists, sex education should start early. When teaching little children to name body parts, do not skip over their private parts as if these were somehow shameful. Teach them the proper names for parts of their body. As time passes, lessons about privacy and boundaries are essential. Preferably, both parents should teach the children that these parts of the body are special, generally not to be touched by or exposed to others, and are never to be discussed in a bad way. As children grow older, they should be informed about the way a man and a woman come together to conceive a child. By the time that their own bodies begin to enter puberty, they should already be well aware of the changes to be expected.

Wise parents help their children to find good friends and then encourage them to enjoy wholesome recreation with them. For many parents, though, this matter of recreation presents challenges of its own. Parents need to set boundaries and restrictions. But more than that, they need to teach their children how to judge what recreation is harmful and to know how much is too much. Such training takes time and effort. Consider an example. A father of two boys noticed that his older son was listening to a new radio station quite frequently. So while driving his truck to work one day, the father tuned in to the same station. Occasionally he stopped and jotted down the lyrics of certain songs. Later he sat down with his sons and discussed what he had heard. He asked questions from their viewpoint, beginning with "what do you think?" and listened patiently to their answers. After reasoning on the matter, the boys agreed not to listen to that station.

Your Family Can Conquer the World: Without question, protecting your family from the world's destructive influences requires much hard work. But there is one thing that, more than any other, will make success possible. It is love! Close, loving family bonds will make your home a safe haven and will promote communication, which is a great protection from bad influences.

Single-Parent Families Can Succeed! One parent families have been called the fastest growing family style in the United States. The situation is similar in many other lands. A record number of divorces, desertions, separations, and illegitimate births have had far-reaching sequences for millions of parents and children.

Being a single parent is like being a juggler. To illustrate my personal experience while growing up in Memphis, Tennessee, my mother was a single parent twenty-one years old, rearing three children alone. She served as mother, father, and provider for my siblings and I. As a youngster I observed first hand the frustration, anger, guilt, and loneliness most single parents face. In light of all the juggling of being a single parent, my mother still reserved quality time for us. She taught us that there were two main ingredients that will always sustain us in life--religion and education and neither should ever be comprised.

Youngsters in single-parent families often have their own struggles. They may have to contend with intense emotions in the wake of a parent's abrupt departure or death. For many youth, the absence of a parent seems to have a profoundly negative effect.

Getting and keeping children active is important for their future health, growth and development. Activity can help enhance self-esteem and confidence, not to mention build healthy bones and lean muscle. As a family, talk to children and find out what interests them. They are more likely to stick with activities that they enjoy. Make or find time for family past times like walking or talking. Make family activities and birthday parties more active by celebrating at parks, home, bowling alleys or skating rinks.

Ask any parent or family member, and they'll say they want to spend more time with their children. Finding the time, however, can be a challenge. Make the most of your time by planning ahead. You don't need a minute-by-minute schedule, but a general outline to get you in the habit of carving out time. Here are some ideas on how to spend meaningful family time together: When you're pressed for time, one way to build togetherness and get things done is to have the entire family work together on household chores. For smaller children, buy child-size tools, like a miniature broom or duster or have them help with a small hand held vacuum. Helping around the house can help your children become more self-sufficient as well.

The family structure serves as a support group for the child or children. It is a reminder and learning experience for the child that this is how they are connected and this is where they came from. A strong family unit is essential to the success of each child's education. The school in conjunction with the family and community must seek to build attitudes that will help raise the quality of family life and strengthen family relationships. So, get the entire family involved in reading books (or favorite parts of books) aloud to each other. As a family, go to the library often. It's free and it has a better selection than any bookstore. For the family, read in unusual places such as under a tree, on the floor, in the park, in a tent, upstairs, or downstairs.

According to Quick Tips, The Parent Institute "Parents are Teachers Too," the family should have "play learning games time". They indicated that family fun time is a great time for learning. Listed below are four examples they cited:

- The Thesaurus Game. Choose a page at random in the Thesaurus. Announce a word. See who can list the most synonyms. Or, take turns with each family member adding a synonym that no one has mentioned.
- Send children on a Scavenger Hunt. List things that are easy to find around the house (something round, something that comes from another country).
- Look at a picture together, one with lots of objects in it. (a catalog collage is good). Then put it away. See who can make the longest list of what was in the picture.
- Cut out newspaper stories and cut off the headlines. Then try to match them with the right stories again. Try writing your

own headlines. Try underlining facts in blue ink, opinions in red (Quick Tips, The Parent Institute, 1995 &1999).

Plan a family hike even if it's through city streets, and pack a blanket and lunch for a picnic. Have a "family art night" once a week. You can work on favorite crafts alongside the child or children who choose and direct their own art activities. As a family, regularly comment on something you genuinely like about the children's work. Point out something interesting an example, some of the colors have blended together to make another color.

Other simple ways to have family fun:
- Play volleyball
- Plan a picnic in the country or local park
- Go to a farmer's market
- Have breakfast together in the backyard
- Play a round of mini golf
- Take a trip to the State or County fair
- Go to church together
- Attend a family reunion together
- Fly kites in the park
- Go fishing
- Go to the movies
- Take walks through the neighborhood and gather rocks and interesting pieces of tree bark.
- Name the animals, insects, trees, and plants you know
- Walk the dog as a family
- Attend outdoor concerts, art and craft fairs
- Play basketball
- Play softball

The family can do good deeds together. The seeds of generous, giving behavior exist in every child, but they need parental family nurturing and guidance to make them grow and flourish. Children who learn generosity tend to have deeper, more meaningful friendships than those who overlook other's needs. This is where the family plays an important role in helping children to understand relationships. As a result of this, children tend to have greater self-esteem from the good feelings that come from making someone else feel good. Family praising displays of generosity, no matter how minor, is a powerful way to encourage such behavior. Families that do good deeds together, not only get the opportunity to spend time together, they share new experiences which can lead to discussions of other important issues.

Helping others can fit into any budget or busy schedule. Many little everyday acts of caring and helpfulness are just as needed as large donations of money or time volunteering. Call a family meeting and decide together what you would like to do to give back to the community. Develop a time table and follow through on your plans.

Even toddlers can learn from family members the true joy of giving. If everyone participates as a family, the efforts will make an even bigger impression on the child or children. Your child or children can sort through toys that they no longer play with, and help to go through closets and drawers to find clothes that are no longer needed. They can then help you take the family's donations to an organization that helps needy families.

On summer days when the weather isn't cooperating, try these great indoor activities as a family:

- Encourage the children to create their own books. Use stamp pads, magazine cut-outs, their own illustrations….whatever they can think of! The children can create a journal of the family life or depict their wildest fantasies. These books should be displayed proudly on their bookshelf along side other "real" books.

- Photos of family fun are too important to hide in a box in the closet. Use a photocopier to enlarge snapshots, and let the children color them in with markers or crayons. Place the works of art on a bulletin board or on the refrigerator. Children can even cut out different people and backgrounds to make fun things. Such activities can give the children a sense of belonging in the family and self-importance to think of themselves as a page in a coloring book.

- The children will be anxious to help decorate for special occasions by making place mats. Use pressed flowers, leaves, and other items found on nature hikes. Create original paper cutouts and affix to construction paper. Laminate the front and back of the mat with clear contact paper.

- Keep a variety of hats, belts, jewelry, and other dress-up accessories on hand. Encourage conversations about the various roles as you and the family, have parties or stage a play.

Source: <u>The Secret of Family Happiness</u> 1996. *Watchtower Bible and Tract Society of New York Inc.* International Bible Students Association, Brooklyn, New York.

In addition, the author suggested seven basic categories of activities for the family to come together and celebrate. The list is as follows:

I. PLAN A FAMILY DAY

<u>What Can We Do As A Family?</u>

Celebrating "Family Day" is a way to reflect on the importance of your role as a parent, whether it be eating dinner with your children or engaging in other family activities. Parents often forget or doubt their ability to positively affect their children's choices, especially their choices concerning substance abuse. Below is a list of activities you can do with your own children on this special day and every day.

➤ Menu planning and preparation for family meals
➤ Taking an active part in homework time
➤ Doing artwork, coloring, or sharing creative activities as a family

➢ Playing board games (checkers, dominos, etc.)
➢ Taking a family walk or bike ride
➢ Reading a story together
➢ Having the family share times of the past, present, and future memories, stories, and dreams
➢ Spend time tape recording elderly family members to document an accurate family history to share with younger family members and future generations
➢ Share and celebrate family successes to enhance family pride, understanding, loyalty, appreciation and positive family contributions.

II. DINNER THEMES

Create a dress-up theme for dinner. Research the theme and dress accordingly at the table. Add props to the room to enhance the experience.

➢ African American
➢ Western
➢ Decades like the 60's
➢ Multicultural
➢ Science Fiction
➢ Sports
➢ Movie Stars
➢ Fictional Characters
➢ Personality Opposites
➢ Heroes and Sheroes
➢ My Favorite Activity – biking, reading, music, etc.
➢ Africa

III. INTERACTIVE RECIPES

Find a recipe in which children can participate in the preparation of the meal. Children can read items from the recipe, have an interactive part in making the dinner, or fully prepare the meal. Such as:

Tacos, Reynolds Wrap Pockets, Grilled Pizza, Pita Sandwiches, English Muffin Pizza, Fruit Kabobs, Pancakes, French Toast, Scrambled Eggs, Pigs in a Blanket, Cupcakes, to name a few.

Create an ethnic theme for the menu and learn about the culture by researching the history of the food and people.

- ➢ Mexican
- ➢ Chinese
- ➢ Southern
- ➢ French
- ➢ Thai
- ➢ Spanish
- ➢ Africa
- ➢ German
- ➢ Indian
- ➢ Hawaiian
- ➢ African American
- ➢ Italian

Theme-Night Activities

➢ Have your children put on a show to tell of items created for the chosen culture.
➢ As parents prepare the meal, children can read about the country from which meals originates, and then the whole family can discuss the country over the meal. Use butcher paper as a tablecloth during the meal for creative writing, drawing, and sharing. Items from the tablecloth can be written down and saved as the "minutes" from dinner that evening.

IV. DINNER TABLE TOPICS

Explore Various Dinner Table Topics…

➢ What is the status of the African American community in America as you see it?
➢ Who are three famous people that you really admire?
➢ Where is one place that you'd really like to visit?
➢ If you were U.S. President, what would you want to change first?
➢ What is one of your most embarrassing moments?
➢ What is the best thing that ever happened to you in school?
➢ What would be your dream job?
➢ What is one of your earliest memories?
➢ What are three gifts you'd like to receive?
➢ What has made you happiest in recent weeks?
➢ Where do you want to be in 10 years?
➢ If you could be one person a day, who would it be?
➢ If you could be any type of animal, which would you choose to be?
➢ If you suddenly became invisible, what would you do first?
➢ What insect or animal frightens you the most?
➢ What is your favorite African American meal?
➢ What is religion to you?
➢ Why is education important?
➢ How would you be successful in this world?
➢ What is Racism?
➢ What is your definition of a family?

V. FAMILY CALENDAR

➢ Plan a family picnic (indoors or outdoors).
➢ Use a calendar to track the number of times in a month that all family members in the household sit down to eat dinner together. The calendar can be used to coordinate schedules to plan future family dinners.

> Schedule a sports activity together.
> Plan a family night of favorite music of family members.
> Plan a family night to discuss family history, roots/ grandparents/great grandparents.
> Plan a family block party.
> Plan a trip to a local college or university, career and technical school.
> Plan a family night of art—use different place settings to make place mats.
> Plan a family game night.
> Plan a church day or night together as a family.
> Plan a trip to a local public school.
> Plan a trip to the family cemetery.
> Plan a trip to a local library, museum and historical sites.

VI. FAMILY DAY

What's It All About

Family Day should be a day to eat dinner with your children in an effort to promote parental engagement as a simple, effective way to raise healthier children. Data also show that teens who often eat dinner with their families are less stressed and bored – two risk factors associated with substance abuse and gang affiliations.

What Does the Data Show?

Since 1966, research has consistently shown that the more often children eat dinner with their families, the less likely they are to be involved in gang related activities, smoking, drinking or using illegal drugs. It's 1998 Teen Survey found that teens who eat dinner with their parents twice a week or less were four times more likely to smoke cigarettes, three times more likely to smoke marijuana and nearly twice as likely to drink and be involved in gang activities than those who ate dinner with their parents six or seven times a week.

84

The following year, the Teen Survey found that teens from families that almost never eat dinner together were 72 percent likelier than the average teen to use illegal drugs, cigarettes, alcohol. They were more deeply involved in gang related activities, became a school drop out or were disinterested in school. While those from families that almost always eat dinner together were 31 percent less likely than the average teen to engage in these activities.

Research by other organizations has shown that teens who eat frequent family dinners are less likely than other teens to have sex at young ages, get into fights or be suspended from school, and are at lower risk for thoughts of suicide. Frequent family dining is also correlated with doing well in school and developing healthy eating habits. This pattern holds true regardless of a teen's sex, family structure, and family socioeconomic level.

Family Day is not just for families. It is a day for all to celebrate, including businesses, unions, religious organizations and community groups. The symbolic act of regular family meals should be promoted and celebrated inside and outside the home throughout the year.

VII. A NATIONAL FAMILY DAY

Designate one day in a month as Family Day – A Day to Eat Dinner With Your Children

WHEREAS the prevention of tobacco, alcohol and drug abuse among young people is, and continues to be, a priority and

WHEREAS the most effective means to prevent and combat substance abuse, addiction, school drop outs and gang related activities lies within the fold of the family; and

WHEREAS parents who remain involved with their children's activities greatly reduce the risk of them dropping out of school, participating in gangs, smoking, drinking or using drugs; and

WHEREAS eating dinner as a family demonstrates and encourages family unity and intercommunication; and

WHEREAS effective communication between family members is conducive to the growth and development of children; and

WHEREAS children from families that almost never eat together, compared to those that do, are over 70 percent more likely to use illegal drugs, cigarettes, alcohol, become deeply involved in gang related activities and become school drop outs or become disinterested in school; and

WHEREAS children from families that almost always eat together are more than 30 percent less likely to use illegal drugs, cigarettes, alcohol, participate in sex or gang related activities or drop out of school;

NOW, THEREFORE, I do hereby extend greetings and best wishes to all observing National Family Day.

Be it Resolved that

1) Responsible parents, grandparents, and concerned adults that eating dinner as a family is an important step toward raising healthy children and;

2) One day in a month shall henceforth be designated A National Family Day – A Day to Eat Dinner with Your Children.

Strong families and strong schools ultimately produce strong and successful children. Family involvement could help their children both at home and at school. When families are involved in their children's education in positive ways, children achieve higher grades and test scores, have better attendance in school, complete more homework. Therefore, families are still the most important influence in their children's lives and they can make a difference in their success or failure.

Two of the deepest, riches words in our language are home and family. May we make them a domain of:

1. Spiritual direction and Prayer
2. Love and Happiness
3. Authority and Discipline
4. Security and Peace
5. Unselfishness
6. Togetherness
7. Helpfulness
8. Counsel and Concern
9. Responsibility
10. Tolerance

When these attitudes prevail, home and family becomes a nest of love, a circle of strength, and a fortress of protection. They can also be a body of togetherness, channel of goodwill, balm of healing, refuge of renewal, school of learning and star of hope. Days come both good and bad, but a strong family is prepared for either. They can enjoy the good ones and handle the bad ones. There is no substitute.

Chapter 4

The Role of Teachers in Rearing Children

"A teacher never stands as tall as when he/she kneels to help a student."

A teacher's greatest contribution is to be sure there is a concerned teacher in every classroom who cares that every student, every day, learns, grows and feels like a real human being. A student will always remember a teacher, good or bad.

In the wake of educational reform, back to the basics, energy crisis, budget cuts, welfare reform, workforce preparedness, integration versus segregation, the educational systems across this country are going through a massive transition on every front. Teachers, as educators, are required to do more with less, raise test scores with limited resources and in many cases, work with students who aren't prepared to take the test.

Teachers are required to be parents, grandparents, teachers, administrators, and extended families with little or no control, appreciation and support. The courts and political pressures have made it almost impossible for teachers to do their job effectively. But, in spite of all these barriers, most teachers in this country have succeeded. Academic excellence in our instructional delivery system should be our number one priority. Teachers exemplify the epitome of quality in our educational system. Teachers are task masters, motivators, leaders, risk takers, survivors and change agents. In many cases teachers have made losers, winners.

Teachers know that the knowledge they have acquired through being formally educated can be powerful, if it is used properly to help teach and educate students. So, teachers should learn everything they can to be able to pass this knowledge on to their students. If students can read, write and compute with clarity and understanding and can articulate the issues of life, they will be successful in this competitive world, if not, they will find themselves even further behind in society.

So, we encourage teachers to continue to fight for what's right in their profession. We ask them to continue to be positive role models for their students and continue to challenge their students and themselves. Students today are being raised at a time when positive role models are rare, and most students view being successful through material things. According to a research study done by The Commission of the States located in Denver, Colorado, most students in today's schools are totally disconnected from society in every arena. So, this is even more of a reason why the role of teacher is so important in helping parents to rear their children.

Role of Teachers

- To look for the good in the parents;
- To consider how their actions would appear to parents i.e., put themselves in their place and ask, "How would a parent feel about this?"
- To think about how parents might be involved in the program and consider if they need to be consulted before a change takes place;
- To help parents understand current education, philosophy and practices;
- To remain supportive of the home in front of the child;
- To send clear information to parents and children about school progress;
- To develop with parents ways they might help their child at home;

- To listen to the parents' point of view and understanding of the child;
- To accept the responsibility for working at school with each child, building on strengths and working on specific needs;
- To treat the parent(s) with respect because they are the parent(s);
- To actively encourage parent participation in their children's learning and in the life of the school;
- To inform parents promptly and specifically about difficulties, both behaviorally and academically;
- To attempt to meet/talk with parents at times convenient for both;
- To be advocates for children;
- To provide positive role models for children;

Botrie and Wenger write in <u>Teachers & Parents Together</u> (1992), on the importance of parental support for schools. In addition, they discussed the roles, perception and attitude plays in how students learn in school. As a result of this, they developed some guiding principles about teachers that are discussed.

Guiding Principles for Teachers

All teachers have beliefs about how students learn and what constitutes optimal learning environments. These beliefs drive the way teachers physically arrange their classrooms, plan their programs, and interact with students. The varied, immediate decisions demanded in teaching require teachers to respond intuitively, based on their own principles of learning. However, the isolation of teaching situations can limit these beliefs about learning from being shared with others. Educators, without opportunities to articulate their beliefs and listen to the experiences of others in their schools, rely on their own motivation to develop professionally. The outcome may be educators with fragmented, polarized educational beliefs operating under the same roof, diminishing one another's effectiveness during the course of a student's progress through the school.

Schools that structure opportunities for teachers to develop and grow provide benefits for all teachers. When teachers within a school collaboratively develop a common set of beliefs about learning, the direction of teaching practice becomes clear and actions more consistent within the school itself.

A much stronger message is sent to parents by schools that collaboratively design policies and programs to reflect the beliefs of parents. This unified message, articulated by teachers and written in policies, offers teachers support when talking with parents. Six teachers, in sequential years, who talk to parents about the social nature of learning create a strong statement. Four teachers who present to parents a workshop on the nature of writing within the school show uniformity. A written set of beliefs about learning that is shared with parents helps them view the school as a cohesive, holistic organization through which their child can move with some consistency. Remember, parents choose schools, not individual teachers. Parental support for a school and its programs is often a matter of perception and attitude. A school that is not in the "top ten" may still be excellent if parents believe that it is.

Schools operate like any organization. The greater the communication between the personnel involved, the greater the chance of strengthening overall effectiveness. Principals who consciously organize these opportunities acknowledge both teachers' individual strengths and their need to grow together. Through the direction of a caring principal, a collaborative school can evolve that utilizes the talents of the personnel inside and outside of the school environment. These school principals establish a positive climate, model a high-energy level, program for all students' success, encourage positive risk-taking, and invite all educational partners to flourish together.

Once these beliefs about learning are established, teachers can more confidently work with parents, knowing that the administration and other teaching staff support them. They can also use these beliefs independently as guideposts when planning for, interacting with, and evaluating students. (Botrie & Wenger pp. 16-17)

Years ago, the teaching profession was the number one profession in our community. Everybody respected the teacher. Everybody wanted to be like their teacher. Whether a person is a dentist, medical doctor, rocket scientist, oceanographer, politician, lawyer or mathematician, she/he could not have been any of those things without spending some quality time with a teacher. We realize that teachers are overworked and underpaid, and in some circles, not even appreciated, however, behind every successful and productive human being, there stands a great teacher. Teachers, as professional educators, have an obligation to expand their student's enthusiasm for learning. I consider our educational system to be better than most, however, if we desire to continue improving, we must continue to strive to be the best, which is why we should celebrate and honor teachers. Teachers truly represent the best in the education profession. Many teachers believe in their students and are always willing to go that extra mile to help a student. Every good teacher dreams of the day a student will surpass them in academic achievement as Plato surpassed Socrates in the times of old.

The teacher is a planner and challenger and may well know that before any worthwhile structure is built, she/he must have a blueprint. As we all know, a blueprint was a plan that charts the future course of action to be taken. It lays the foundation upon which the building must rest as long as it lasts. The blueprint, along with the specifications, determines the kind of material that must go into the structure, in this case, academic excellence. It determines, as you must determine, what kind of things your life will be made of. Will the lumber of your life be green and buckle at life's slightest adversity? Will the sub-flooring of your life be so weak as to topple with the slightest wind of trouble? Teachers, will the doors to your life be closed to adventure and change? Will the polish and wax of a teacher's life soon lose its gloss? Will the brick of a teacher's life lose its mortar and crumble suddenly? Will the roof of a teacher's life spring a leak and allow misguided deeds, like water, to run like a mighty flood?

A teacher's blueprint of academic excellence calls for lumber tried and tested. Lumber that gives and sways with adversity, but rises to the cause of self-respect. It calls for sub-flooring like the Rock of Gibraltar, strength of purpose and willingness to succeed while others predict failure. It calls for doors that stand forever ajar to the beautiful, wonderful world of knowledge. It calls for a polish of beautiful gold that shines the radiance of hope all around you. For teachers, this blueprint calls for mortar that will not crack or crumble, but with resolute conviction of the writer who said: "I'm wounded, but not slain. I shall lie here and bleed awhile, and then get up and fight again". This blueprint calls for the totality of a teacher's life to be like a roof covering, to offer shelter and protection to the weak and oppressed wherever you find them. Teachers must continue their desires and efforts to help students accomplish their goals and to graduate as confident, productive, and life long learners. Learners who clearly understand their relationship with society and the world along with the possession of appropriate skills, attitudes, and abilities will be successful. As a result of teachers' support, and with hard work, and dedication, their students will continue to reach and exceed their goals.

Some of my teachers and coaches from Frederick Douglass High School in Memphis, Tennessee, Mrs. Theresa Shannon, Mrs. Geraldine Little, Coach Albert Miller and Coach William Little, may have expressed their final ambition in these words: "If I were standing to be judged before the Great White Throne, where I could hear the righteous sing and hear the sinners moan...I'd want no finer advocate to make my final plea, than some boy or girl who would say: 'Gee, that teacher did a lot for me!'" Now that you have read the blueprint of what an outstanding teacher is--I would like to leave a simple challenge with all teachers. Teachers, continue to stand up for what's right with your students, even if you have to stand alone. Continue to be a positive role model for your students. Continue to challenge them and to challenge yourself. Remember as teachers, you hold the key to the future in your hands—your students. As teachers, you are the ones that will develop the future leaders of tomorrow. Teachers are the ones that will develop the teachers, business leaders, politicians, and the medical doctors who will find the cure for Diabetes, Heart Disease, AIDS, and Cancer. So, we ask teachers to stay strong, stay focused, stay true to their convictions, and true to their profession.

As a career educator for Pre-K-16 schools, my definitions of a good and dynamic teacher are listed as follows:

➢ **A good teacher has a love of learning and an intense liking of the students they teach**. A love of learning is contagious for all the students. A good teacher truly feels that all the students in his/her class can and will learn. Students learn best if they know their teacher cares about their success and has worked hard to provide lessons that are fun, challenging and enjoyable.

➢ **A good teacher is prepared**. Every minute of the class period is filled with a variety of activities. Teacher-directed instruction, questioning, discussion, group activity, and evaluation are important parts of effective lessons. The lesson plans have clear and precise objectives that are measurable. These objectives state clearly what the teacher expects the students to know or be able to do as a result of the lesson. To be a good teacher requires a lot of time outside the classroom preparing for the classroom experience.

➢ **Good teachers get good results**. Every student will show some progress and a large percentage are successful. Success breeds success. Negative attitudes are not allowed in the classroom of a good teacher. Good teachers experience many more successes, and the students are excited at seeing themselves and the teacher as successful. Every teacher wants to be an effective teacher. Every teacher knows down deep whether he/she is being successful, being marginally successful, or is not being successful at all. Sometimes egos get in the way of seeking help or being willing to admit a lack of effectiveness on the part of the teacher.

➢ **All teachers can improve** and must work at recognizing those areas that need to be strengthened. Every teacher must work to improve each year. The good teacher never stops learning and trying new and different strategies to make his/her classroom an exciting learning experience for all students.

➢ **Dynamic Teaching is effective teaching**. It encompasses the various strategies an effective teacher uses to teach students. When teaching is dynamic, it is exciting, interesting, innovative and very effective in achieving learning by students. A teacher who seeks new and diverse methods to keep students clamoring to know more and more about a subject is dynamic. Dynamic instructors are creative in presenting subject matter, making the subject relevant to the life of students and develops in them a love for life-long learning. Students become independent learners as a result of such teaching. They seek learning on their own. The teacher becomes more of a coach guiding the independent seeking of knowledge by the students. Students are anxious to come to the classes of these dynamic teachers. They are excited about all the new information they learn and want to share with their friends, parents and other teachers. The students become involved and immerse themselves in the subject. They don't need to be pushed to further investigate ideas. They volunteer for projects and extra assignments because they love to learn.

In order to have dynamic teachers, schools will have to be sure they select only the finest candidates for the position. Teachers should be selected who have impeccable credentials from reputable colleges and universities. They are persons who are life-long learners themselves, who enjoyed school and learning. It's important to employ teachers who are very competent and love the subject they are prepared to teach. Also, hire persons who are not inhibited, but outgoing, curious, and creative. These dynamic teachers should be compensated fairly and schools should not be shy about publicly praising their accomplishments.

To enhance dynamic teaching several ideas may be instituted. Staff development by a dynamic teacher will inspire those who have fallen into the same boring presentations of their subject. Visitations to classes where dynamic teaching is in progress will give teachers ideas they can explore for their own classrooms. Encouraging and openly supporting innovative teaching methods will lay the groundwork for other teachers to try something new in their classrooms. Award ceremonies, newspaper articles highlighting creative teachers, interviews with motivated students, and other means of recognition may cause teachers to take a critical look at their own classes. Seminars and workshops also provide inspiration and ideas for teachers.

Perhaps the most effective tool for creating dynamic teaching is high expectations. When a high expectation for dynamic teaching is the rule, all instructors will seek to reach those expectations. The groundwork for such expectation must come from the administration. When it is known that only those teachers who are exceptional will be hired, the pool of applicants is likely to be only from the best schools of education. A reputation for having only dynamic teachers on staff must be earned by setting high expectations and then monitoring the performances of the teachers. Encourage, support, motivate, provide in-service, staff development, seminars, and conferences, celebrations of success, and generous compensation to dynamic teachers and others will imitate them.

Furthermore, to enhance the role of teachers in public education, Siobhan McDonough of the Associated Press wrote an article titled, "Study Reveals Top Education Concerns" (April 23, 2003, Washington Post). It was a survey on educational standards discussed by teachers, parents, and students' educational concerns in public schools. Ill mannered pupils, demoralized teachers, uninvolved parents and bureaucracy in public schools are greater worries for Americans than the standards of accountability that occupy policymakers, a new study says.

Teachers, parents and students said they were concerned about the rough-edged atmosphere in many high schools, according to the report released by Public Agenda, a research and policy organization in New York City. Only 9 percent of surveyed Americans said the students they see in public are respectful toward adults. High school students were asked about the frequency of serious fights in the schools and 40 percent said they hardly ever happened; 4 percent had no opinion. Only 1 percent of teachers said teacher moral is good in their high school. This is a true reflection of how the public feels. It says that our young people are looking for positive role models out there.

The report, drawing together more than 25 surveys done by Public Agenda, traces how attitudes of parents, teachers, students, principals, employers and college professors have changed over the last 10 years. A typical national random sample telephone survey on standards in 2000 canvassed 803 parents of public school pupils in grades K-12, with a margin of error of plus or minus 3 percentage points. The report says standard testing is important, but many other factors are hurting academic performance.

The 2001 No Child Left Behind Act holds schools accountable for student achievement. States must devise and offer tests in reading and mathematics for every child each year in grades three through eight, beginning in the fall 2005. Under current law, states are required to test pupils in reading and math three times during their K-12 years. The standards movement has taken hold in American schools and continues to enjoy broad support. But there are some troublesome fault lines,

Teachers "believe in higher standards but often feel they can't count on students to make the effort or parents and administrators to back them up." Superintendents and principals want more autonomy over their schools, with 81 percent of superintendents and 47 percent of principals saying talented leaders most likely will leave because of politics and bureaucracy.

Teachers said their views are generally ignored by decision-makers with 70 percent feeling left out of the loop in their district's decision-making process. According to the report, 73 percent of employers and 81 percent of professors said public school graduates have fair or poor writing skills. Teachers said lack of parental involvement is a serious problem, with 78 percent of teachers saying too many parents don't know what's going on with their child's education.

In the report titled Aches in Education released by Public Agenda on standards in 2000 teachers, parents and students voiced their concerns with public schools. "The Aches in Education" are:

1. Their local schools have serious problems with lack of student discipline: 76%
2. Fighting, violence and gangs: 63%

Teachers Say:
1. My school puts obstacles in my way when I'm trying to accomplish goals at work: 67%
2. Parents who refuse to hold their kids accountable for their behavior or academic performance are a serious problem: 81% (McDonough, 2003)

As a teacher, the author suggests ten statements listed below as effective approaches to enhance student's achievements:

"TEACHERS, TOUCH A CHILD, TOUCH THE FUTURE, TO REACH ALL, TEACH ALL"

1. **EXPECT RESPECT:** Administrators, faculty, staff, and students: take responsibility for ensuring equity.

2. **REFLECT RESPECT:** Reflect diversity in choosing leaders and honoring students and faculty.

3. **LEARN TO TEACH DIFFERENCE:** Learn about and teach to both genders, various cultures and ethnicity, different learning styles and abilities.

4. **LET THEM SEE WHAT THEY CAN BE:** Provide past and present role models in textbooks, media and lectures. Show both females and males various cultures, ethnicity and abilities.

5. **CONSIDER ALL TO HEAR FROM EACH:** Encourage and appreciate every student's contribution to classroom discussion and activities. No taunting, teasing or harassing.

6. **ALLOCATE TO ACCOMMODATE:** Budget money and resources fairly and inclusively.

7. **TEST TO GET EACH STUDENT'S BEST:** Assess achievement in varying ways to give all students a chance to shine. Multiple intelligences and individual experiences require multiple modes of evaluation.

8. **SEPARATE TO EVALUATE**: Analyze data by gender and ethnicity to gauge whether subgroups are taught adequately and test scores improve over time.

9. **PLACE NO BANS ON DREAMS AND PLANS:** Don't stereotype! Counsel and enroll students according to their interests, abilities, and dreams.

10. **EQUITIZE THEIR WHOLE LIVES:** Establish partnerships with parents, employers, and the community to promote educational equity.

An article written by Mr. Thad Rueter, on March 16, 2003 in the Daytona Beach, Florida News-Journal stated the following: "Poorer and minority students end up with less-experienced teachers and schools in less-affluent areas are in a fight for a few good teachers. The whitest, most affluent schools tend to have teachers with more experience, education and subject expertise than schools serving poor and minority neighborhoods." In my response, I commended Mr. Thad Rueter, staff writer for the Daytona Beach, Florida News-Journal, for producing such a well-written article that addressed a serious problem this country faces with public education. Teacher preparation and training have been my area of expertise for the past 30 years. I have been a dean of teacher education at two historically and predominately Black universities, Fayetteville State University in Fayetteville, North Carolina and the University of the District of Columbia in Washington, D.C. I have seen first hand teacher preparation and training effective in preparing teachers to teach children of color in poor schools. It can be done and it has been done in the past. But we have to be committed to make sure all children can and will have an opportunity to learn. The greatest challenge and contribution for every concerned citizen and teacher should be to see that there is a competent, qualified, compassionate, concerned, tolerant and patient teacher in every classroom. A good teacher is one who cares that every student, every day, learns, grows, and feels like a real human being, and assures that no child is left behind in the teaching and learning process.

The article eluded to the fact that well-trained teachers with expertise are not assigned to poor and majority black or non-white schools. This is true throughout this country in every urban, inner city, poor and majority black school system. Why? The answer is obvious. We don't really want to educate the masses of poor, black and non-white children in this country. We aren't serious about preparing our young people (poor and black or non-white) for the future. We have more of everything in our schools today, but fewer and fewer students of color are learning. The school drop out rate has more than doubled in the past 10 years in public schools throughout this country.

We have no one to blame but ourselves. We invest more money into preparing for war than we do in teaching our children to learn and to be productive citizens. We have created a dual system of learning in this society. The poor are getting poorer and the rich are getting richer. Only about 10 to 20% of children of color are being properly trained and educated. I am concerned about the 75 to 80% of our children who are left behind and who will grow up in a society where they cannot make a positive contribution in life or to society. The prison system is growing by leaps and bounds while the educational system sinks lower and lower.

Having better trained and prepared teachers with experience alone is not the answer. It is part of the answer. There are thousands of well trained and prepared teachers teaching in our schools every day across the country with many years of experience who cannot teach children of color in our urban, poor, and inner city schools systems. They have not been properly trained to teach students of color. They have no clue what to do with these non-white children. They cannot relate to them nor understand why the children are so different from the way they (the teachers) were raised and educated. These students of color look, act, learn and respond to the teaching and learning process differently than the training the teacher received at the college or university.

A good teacher-training program trains potential teachers for the area of the community in which the new teacher will be working. This is a must if we are going to be successful in teaching the masses of students of color in our school systems throughout this country. An excellent resource for training teachers to teach in urban, poor school systems is taught at the University of Central Florida (UCF) in Orlando, Florida. This program is under the direction of Dr. Martha Lue, a professor in the College of Education. UCF has developed an 18-graduate semester hour Certificate in Urban Education. This program of study addresses different cultures, races, teaching techniques, modalities and styles of learning to assist teachers who teach in urban school systems. Teachers need to know, appreciate and understand the students they are teaching in order to be effective in the classroom.

So, the role of a teacher in the teaching learning process of a child is important and crucial to the child's total development. Children learn all the time. They learn from others. They learn by listening, watching and doing. So, the teacher will become a new and important adult in your child/children's life. Therefore, a teacher, parent, school, and community partnership is vital in assisting your child to learn. This partnership will enable the child to receive well-rounded support that is needed for children to be stable and productive in life.

As a former teacher, my own classroom experiences, observations, and personal growth throughout the teaching years have clearly demonstrated to me, that the teaching profession encounters many daily challenges. As a result, we need to dialogue often with other teachers and consider other parents as collaborative partners if parents and our students are to thrive.

Chapter 5

The Role of Religion in Rearing Children

"Faith gives hope, broadens horizons, and heals the soul"

It is difficult to express the role religion plays in rearing children since religion is such a sensitive issue in today's society. The author will take the approach of citing examples and quoting case studies about religious principles and practices surrounding religion and education. In some cases, the author will use the word "God and Supreme Being" interchangeably to give the reader another approach when reading religious statements and quotations.

The courts and society have not yet agreed on how religion should or shouldn't be practiced or displayed in school; but the religious beliefs of parents have a great deal of impact on rearing children. It affects behavior patterns, discipline, customs, and value systems. As a result of all these crucial factors, parents need to be careful not to take their religious practices and principles to the extreme and always give their child or children a balanced upbringing. Having strong beliefs in religion and education with some families have been the two main ingredients that have sustained their family life and structure.

One of my spiritual advisors, the late Rev. Dr. E. D. Butler, former pastor of Second Missionary Baptist Church in Bloomington, Indiana shared his beliefs about religion, parents, and education in rearing children in one of his Sunday sermons as follows:

There are concerns the family must deal with. When our Supreme Being from the brow of the Mount of Olives wept over the city of Jerusalem, He was expressing deep social concern. When He cleansed the Temple, He was engaged in social action. When He died on the Cross, He was revealing and paying the cost of individual, family, and social regeneration and reconciliation. When by His very life He vanquished death, He was assuring the total victory that can come to the families of the world that is our Supreme Being's plan of redemption.

The family today has an inescapable appointment with the question of social justice, and all of us are involved. Many of us are experiencing a radical revolution for which we have not been prepared. Racial relations are undergoing a change that brings tension as hope. Where does the family fit into such an hour?

Now don't be angry with me from the beginning, but the question that often comes to me is what business is it of ours? Well, the only answer I can give is also a question. What is the business of the family, the family of our Supreme Being, the Church?

During the officers training session recently, I came across the acronyms R.S.T.S. (Reach to Save, Teach to Serve). This is the families' business and the business of the church, which is His Body. The first business of the Church which is the family of our Supreme Being is to reach out into the community and save souls, but this action must begin at home. The Gospel is the only saving agent that the world knows but maybe we need to look at what we mean by saving souls? Do social conditions have anything to do with the souls of persons, with what happens to them as persons? Have you really thought that the real test of our social decision is what happens to our children? No social problem is just a problem in general, but becomes a condition that leaves it mark upon our children. How can we forget what social injustices do to children on all sides.

If there is any condition in which people live that endangers souls, especially children, who can escape the responsibility of doing something? True, no one is ever saved by a better social condition. One is saved only by the Grace of our Supreme Being. Can it be that our hands and hearts be the means of our Supreme Being's

Grace in helping a child find a better condition in which to grow up? Preaching the gospel and the saving of souls is the business of the church and this must begin in the family.

Our Supreme Being gave the deepest command and gave the greatest motive for a human that is to love his /her Supreme Being with all their heart, mind, soul, and strength and one's neighbor as one's self. In the family at home, this love must include all members. Every believer is called to practice love. Yes, our Supreme Being calls us to the obedience in the command to love, and in this context must see every man or person as one of great worth. It means affirming the oneness of the human family everywhere. If our Supreme Being is our Father, we are all His children. If we are not His, then He is not the Father of any of us. We are all tied together in the family with all the adjustments.

Now there are certain patterns of behavior that go with the acts of love for all of love is relational. That is why our Supreme Being taught us that the central issue in life today must be that we love our Supreme Being. For without love for our Supreme Being, there can be no love at all and nothing else really matters. It is extremely difficult to define or describe love for the Divine for our children. For it is bound in our understanding of it. Love's brilliance and beauty are expressed and experienced in ways as varied as there are people. For some of us it is an emotional experience, just a wink across the room could send a message and flutter a heart. Red roses can say much. Saying that love defies description does not mean that we are left to love any old way we please. Love does have boundaries. When parents love their children they find ways to discipline. Every child loves to know that someone cares enough to tell him/her right from wrong.

When our Supreme Being taught that we were to love Him, the words used help us to understand how. Loving our Supreme Being is about surrendering, yielding, obedience. It is about giving all of ourselves. When we do this consistently, our Supreme Being knows we love Him. Our Supreme Being has given parents in the family opportunities and responsibilities that when carried out, demonstrate love. Just providing food and shelter does not of itself express love. But to parents, sharing of self and the love for your Supreme Being with your children is vital in assisting you in rearing well rounded children. There is a richness to love that we must pursue if we are to have love's full benefits. While our Supreme Being's word sets clear boundaries for our love to Him, there is a target within the boundary that deserves our aim. Its like archery, the goal is not just to stay within the circle, but to zero in on the bull's eye.

Our real need for our Supreme Being is fulfilled when living our love for Him in dutifully yielding. He comes to us with Grace and Truth. For love is not only an opportunity or responsibility, it must be a response. Our need for our Supreme Being comes home in the fact that without Him we can do nothing. We as family members have the problem of so quickly losing sight of the Glory of our Supreme Being and the marvelous grace that He showers on our lives daily. I heard a woman say the other day, "If He never does another thing, He is worthy of all my praises." If He never does anything more than rescue us from hell and give us the guidance and ability to help rear our children, He has already done more than we deserve. As the songwriter affirms "Love so amazing, so Divine, demands my life, my soul, my all." (Sermon of Dr. Butler, March, 2000).

Religion played an important role in assisting school and parents in educating and rearing children the 1950's and 1960's as I grew up in Memphis, Tennessee and attended public school, grades 1-12. We had daily prayer in school during the morning followed by the pledge of allegiance to the flag. To most of us, this religious ritual was an extension of our home environment. So, as children, we really didn't give this religious process a second thought! We grew to accept and respect it.

As a career educator, observing the behavior of children and the deplorable conditions of our schools across America, I am a firm believer that when prayer and discipline were taken out of the schools, we lost the children. We lost our values, structure, pride, standards and commitment.

When I attended public school, I viewed religion in the school as giving me structure, a strong belief system, guiding principles, and stability. This was certainly something nurturing and long lasting, because I still adhere to these religious principles and practices today, some fifty years later.

Therefore, from my viewpoint, the role religion plays in school is appropriate as long as you don't impose ones religious beliefs on another. Having the choice to say yes or no or to choose should be left up to the individual not the group.

Charles Rohn's article titled, Plenty of Religious Expression in Public Schools (May/June 2001, Illinois School Board Journal) stated how confusing rules are in our school system pertaining to religion and education. His comments are as follows:

I recently visited an adult Sunday school class where the discussion turned to religion and the public schools. Among the statements I heard were these:.

- Schools would not have discipline problems if prayer were allowed.
- A student cannot even say grace in the cafeteria.
- Students are not allowed to have a Bible study club at school.
- Students are not permitted to circle the flagpole for prayer.
- When I was a student we were taught right and wrong. Today's students don't know where rules come from.
- All of our troubles in public schools started when they kicked God out!

Many of those in the class had children in the public schools. They contended the faith they hold so dear could not be expressed in today's schools. They believed school staff may not carry their religious beliefs with them into the public schools. These parents, not unlike others, were wrong about the role of religious faith in the public schools.

CONFUSING RULES

Expression of religious beliefs in the public schools is a controversial issue. Numerous court cases have caused confusion concerning exactly what place religion has in our schools. School leaders must combine a general understanding of recent rulings with a large dose of common sense to avoid problems.

Are students allowed to pray in school? A bumper sticker states "As Long as There Are Tests, There Will Be Prayer in Schools." Students can pray in public schools, either as individuals or in groups. They can pray before a test, lunch, a ballgame or before the start of classes. However, their prayers cannot be disruptive or infringe on others' rights. Long-established standards require that prayers be voluntary and that school employees not lead or publicly participate in the prayers.

Should a school activity be opened with prayer? Many schools traditionally have opened graduation ceremonies, athletic events and other activities with prayer led by a student or a local minister. Current legal standards no longer allow this type of prayer. Recent court cases have been numerous, and the U.S. Supreme Court shortly is expected to rule on prayer by students at a school sporting event. What is clear is that school officials cannot organize, initiate or encourage public prayer. But for the moment, student-initiated, student-led prayer during a time of meditation or reflection is legal.

Can teachers share their faith? The example that teachers set for their students speaks much louder than words. Teachers have a captive audience, therefore, they are not allowed to change or encourage students to accept specific religious beliefs. Children have an uncanny ability to clearly see what adults believe from their actions. A teacher who quietly exhibits religious beliefs in his or her daily life will provide a positive example for students.

Should student religious activities be held on school property? Many schools allow students to organize and meet for religious purposes on school property. This common activity is legal if done properly. The basic standards that must be met are that students must organize the activity, it must be voluntary and it cannot conflict with regular school activities. If the school has established a limited open forum by allowing the scouts, chess club or other non-academic organizations to meet on school property, the Bible club also must be allowed to meet. Students across the country are meeting at their school to study the Bible and even to pray at the flagpole.

Are public school students permitted to read the Bible? Students do not leave their rights at the schoolhouse door. A student has a right to privately read materials but does not have the right to coerce other students to read or listen. Recent rulings have supported a student's rights to select religious materials for personal and private reading within the school building. A teacher, however, may refuse to allow a student to select religious materials for an assignment in order to meet the requirements of that assignment or to provide for the reading of a desired variety of materials.

In other words, a student may read a Bible or religious information privately during free time or if it is acceptable as reading material or resource for an assignment. But a student who continually chooses the Bible or other religious materials as the only source for book reports in every class may not be able to do so because teachers may require a broader scope of literature to be covered.

Can ministers be allowed on school property? Many ministers are involved with community activities that take place outside their churches. Many volunteer by reading to elementary students, supervising high school dances, tutoring students, coaching sports and serving on committees. Ministers have been called upon to be counselors to schoolchildren during a crisis situation. In these roles ministers and rabbis do not change or verbalize their faith, they share their faith by living it. Ministers, as all other adults, can share their faith with youth both in and out of public schools primarily by living those beliefs.

Community Expression

The basic question has been, "Must public schools be ungodly places?" The answer is an emphatic "NO." Religious beliefs play an important part in the education of our children. The laws and court cases have placed limitations on expressions of one's beliefs including our religious beliefs. However, religion and God can still be a part of rearing children and having them attend public schools.

The dramatic court cases, the outlandish situations and the major tragedies grab the focus of our news media and often make us believe the worst about our society and its youth. A community's religious beliefs can and should be a part of the education of children. As long as educational leaders and teachers understand current standards and use common sense, there is no problem with the values of the community being expressed in public schools (Rohn, www.iasb. com).

What Does the Bible Say About Parenting?

1. Respect and honor is due to parents.
2. Parents should have a good strong relationship with God.
3. Parents have a responsibility to teach children.
4. Discipline is a part of the child rearing process.
5. Parents (adults) have the responsibility to care, love and protect the younger generation.
6. Parents have authority to be parents, yet they should respect children.
7. Parents should encourage the younger generation.

Is one's religion related to preferred child-rearing techniques? This is an age old question many parents believe is true when it comes to the kind of disciplinary decisions they make about how to discipline their children. Some parents believe that prayer is the answer and others believe in some form of punishment or discipline.

As an old saying, "spare the rod, you spoil the child" or Proverbs 22:6 states, "train up a child in the way he should go, when he is old, he will never depart from it."

Having helped to rear four children myself, I can truly say that our religious beliefs and practices were significant in assisting my four children in being productive and caring human beings. We tend to learn from others and I was taught my religious values and beliefs from my mother and grandfather. These same religious values, I passed on to my children. My mother, stepfather and grandfather instilled in me that there are two main ingredients that will sustain you in life. These two main ingredients are "religion and education" and they should never be comprised.

I can remember my first teaching assignment, 1967, a middle school in Sikeston, Missouri. In this Bible belt, impoverished cotton southern town near the Kentucky, Arkansas and Illinois borders, religious beliefs were instilled in every household, rich, poor, black or white. During my teaching tenure in Sikeston, my living quarters were one room furnished which was part of a rooming house owned and operated by Mr. & Mrs. Frances Troupe. My monthly rent was $40 for room and board and one long distant telephone call. Most people in this small country southern town attended some form of church.

Religion was an integral part of the curriculum at Sikeston Middle School. This concept was a continuous process from school to home and home to school. School and church were a vital part of children's communities and daily lives. In those days, the two seemed to work extremely well together in helping to rear children.

Because of the many changes in laws governing religion and education, I think it should be left up to parents to introduce religion to their children. This is crucial since parents have different religious beliefs, customs, traditions, and styles.

Being a parent is an expensive and heavy responsibility, because a parent's influence is a child's "copy book". Parents, if we want children to be honest, we should be honest. If we want them to be truthful, we should be truthful, never tell a lie. If we want them to be sensitive to the needs of others, let them see us help the sick, destitute, and downtrodden. If we want to guard them from becoming alcoholics, don't drink before them. If we want them to be self-supporting, teach them to work. If we want children to be law-abiding citizens, we must demand obedience. If we want them to go to church, take them. Children learn from the adults around them. John Locke states, "parents wonder why the streams are bitter when they themselves have poisoned the fountain."

Chapter 6

The Role of School in Rearing Children

"Quality instruction and satisfied students are our number one priority in schools"

The school has long been the focal point in assisting parents in rearing children. In some states, the child or children see the school as an extended family or a great place to feel safe and a great place to learn. This is done through free breakfast and lunch programs as well as after school organized and structured programs. After all, most children in schools in the United States, spend at least 6 hours a day at school under some form of supervised instruction. So, school plays an important role in rearing children. With parents and schools working together as partners, the role of school in rearing children will be more clearly defined.

As a career educator who started teaching in 1967 at a middle school in Sikeston, Missouri, I had no clue the role school had if any, in helping parents to rear children. I simply thought that all parents had an excellent working relationship with schools across America. This perception was based on the fact of how I was reared in Memphis, Tennessee and Hernando, Mississippi's public schools.

Reared in a segregated community and school system, things seemed to be very simple, precise and less complicated. There is an old saying "what you don't know will never hurt you." These educational environments were great learning experiences for me in learning how to appreciate and understand the role of school and how it was connected to family and community. In those days, we had what I called "a school/community concept."

Born in Hernando, Mississippi, a little country town some twenty miles south of Memphis, Tennessee, I had the good fortune to attend school in segregated settings in Memphis and Mississippi all year around. Learning was contagious to me as a child. I was involved in the year-round school concept in the fifties and sixties before the concept was popular in educational circles. My brother Jesse and I would attend public school in Memphis, Tennessee from September to May and in Hernando, Mississippi from May to September. Schools in Hernando were seasonal schools, only in session when the cotton crops weren't ready to be chopped or picked. Therefore, we attended school all year-round. As a result of this continuous teaching and learning process, my brother and I grew to thoroughly enjoy school and clearly understood its role. During our upbringings, the role of the school was to serve as a place to greet, meet, learn, see positive role models, socialize, and be a home away from home support group environment. School and church were the center of a child's life. They were the only real viable outlets for us to learn while having fun. In those days, you didn't have too many options and this worked extremely well for my brother Jesse and me. Our parents knew where we were at all times because there were only two places to go in Hernando, Mississippi and Memphis, Tennessee, church and school. In most cases, the church and school were directly across the road from each other. Therefore, everything we were exposed to in our school/church settings were positive. This nurturing school environment developed character, good self esteem, self confidence, pride, one's appreciation of his/her own history and the understanding of the role of the school in acquiring knowledge and skills.

The role of school in assisting parents in rearing their children is one of vital importance. But an even more important role is for parents to teach their children about all of the pitfalls they will encounter while attending school. Therefore, teaching children about the realities of life in school goes far beyond reading, writing, and computing.

Teaching children about the realities of life, A,B,C,D'S, the author calls it knowing "The Hidden Rules of Life." This is what I refer to as, "Knowing the System for What it is Worth." We tell children to study hard, stay in school, make good grades and they will be successful in life. But, the truth is, if they don't have a clear and concise understanding of how the system of life works and knowing what I call "the pecking order," poor people and people of color will never be successful in this world.

An approach and message to our children is to always adhere to my 5 P's of life, <u>Prior, Planning, Prevents, Poor, Performance</u>. In addition, always have plan A,B, C, and D to be able to address the pitfalls and disappointments of life. People will stress you out, disappoint you, let you down, discourage you, dislike you, irritate you and cause you pain and agony. How does a mother equip a child to deal with these pitfalls of life? By following my plan A, B, C, and D of life, as a parent you should say to your child/children the following:

- Plan A - Try not to ever put yourself in a position where you always have to rely on another human being.

- Plan B- Always create/make alternative plans or options in life.

- Plan C- There is no price tag on experience and exposure. So, get all the experience and exposure you can get in life.

- Plan D- Never compromise your principles.

In a school setting, who should be held responsible for causing these pitfalls to a child? Who should be held accountable? This is crucial to know because children are vulnerable, extremely fragile, and emotional. Not knowing "The Hidden Rules" of the reality of life, the child will act out, get in trouble in school or become withdrawn. This behavior pattern feeds into the hands of the teacher or adult who is causing disruption in the child's life by creating these pitfalls.

Stress in public school classrooms is at an all time high. It comes in many forms. Some of it is intentional and deliberately aimed at children of color. There is no school curriculum that exists addressing how students should deal with stress in the classroom.

In all fairness to the teachers, in some cases, the teaching and learning environment in poor and poverty stricken public schools is not very conducive to learning. The condition of the school environment does not excuse any teachers' ill treatment of students. But, if it goes unnoticed, it will escalate and the child will always suffer. It is the role of the parent, grandparent or significant family member to address this problem. Parents, grandparents or significant family members should be constant visitors at their children's school. They should be observers, listeners, and participants in their children's school.

Parents, grandparents or significant family members, if they are visiting their children's school on a regular basis, these are some of the pitfalls they can observe and/or prevent their children or child from experiencing in school:

- Sarcasm
- Favoritism
- Racism
- Discouragement
- Lack of attention
- Being ignored
- Exclusion
- Isolation
- Rude and or disrespectful treatment
- Low expectations
- Bullying

This is why parents, grandparents, and or significant family members need to know and be aware of what their role is as it relates to the school. Not knowing your role and rights as a parent, grandparent and/or significant family member will have a negative impact on your children.

Parents, grandparents, or significant family members should lead by example. When a parent has poor eating habits, the child will develop poor eating habits. Proper diet and exercise are key elements to good health, having a stable child and longevity in life. With a sound body and mind, a child will be better prepared to learn. Therefore, parents, grandparents, or significant family members should try to do the following:

- Eat healthy, get plenty of sleep, exercise, drink plenty water, no smoking or drugs.

- Spend time with your child where the child is the focus of your attention, either in discussions about the future, events of today, or engage in playing non–electronic games that involve conversation and an exchange of ideas. Meditate, play, and pray with them.

- Be honest with your children and always have an open dialogue.

- Praise your children. Love them, protect them and lead by example.

So, parent, grandparents, or significant family members, *"Save Our Children, Save Our Schools, Never, Ever Give Up On Our Children, because our Children are our greatest resource, our Children are an extension of us, and our Children are our future"*.

Authors Maureen Botrie and Pat Wenger's book titled Teacher and Parents Together, Markham, Ontario, Pembroke Publishers Limited/ Portland, Maine, Stenhouse Publishers, 1992. The following is from the article titled Today's Child in Tomorrow's World.

As we move into the 21st century, educators and parents need to thoughtfully envision the kinds of skills, behaviors, and values children will need in order to function successfully in the future. If we determine what kind of products we are working to create in the schools and in our homes, based on what children will need, then the kind of experiences our students should have become clearer.

Parents and educators in each school might want to identify their views around this question. We believe children will need practice during their childhood to develop:

- Critical thinking and problem solving skills.
- Strong skills in all communication modes (oral and written), and in science and mathematics.
- The ability to function in a multiculturally, diverse democratic society.
- The ability to be a productive worker, committing energy towards quality and service.
- A striving for and recognition of excellence.
- An awareness of the fragility of the environment.
- An appreciation of aesthetics through experiences with art and music.
- Comfort with technology.
- The ability to access information.
- Positive attitudes toward preventative health and physical fitness
- Social and community responsibilities.
- Confidence to accept responsibility for their own decision
- Positive values within a complex, evolving world.
- How to work well with others in a group setting to accomplish a task.
- Appreciate their responsibility for community service.

By strengthening our partnership between home and school, we create a safety net of success for children, and strong support that will guide them throughout their childhood and adolescence. Our collaborative efforts should help children to be well equipped to enter the next century with self-assurance and anticipation (Botrie & Wenger p. 143).

From advisor to equal partner, from passive listener to decision maker--indeed, from fundraiser to hell-raiser--the role of parents in schools is changing. Parents are becoming more vocal about being involved in education decision making. The family is becoming important as an instructional partner. Market-based education initiatives, such as charter schools and voucher programs, are changing parents from citizens to customers.

School leaders can no longer view parents as appendages to schooling or meddlers in their work. They can no longer ignore parents or treat them with disdain. Without community support, education reform will not survive and the future of civic responsibility toward education is in danger. School systems across the country have created a number of educational programs for parents, children and schools to work together. Many school systems across this country have included in their operating budgets professional parent advocates. These advocates have played a vital role in assisting parents and schools in rearing and educating children.

The Role of Parents With a Paid Advocate

This is a person who would go out into the neighborhood and encourage parents to come into the school and get more involved in the child's school life. This parent advocate would work with parents one at a time, showing each parent specifically how to get involved. They would demonstrate for the parent what to do and how to do it. The parent advocate would be a support system for each parent, solving whatever problem the parent had for getting involved in their child's education at school. This might be transportation, babysitting, motivation, fear of the school environment and education itself because they had poor experiences with school themselves. The parent advocate would help with the parent's employer, to get them time off to be involved with the child's school activities, such as, parent conferences, field trips, school plays or programs, PTA or PTO meetings, school advisory council meetings that may be held during the day and regular volunteer hours.

The parent advocate would monitor daily the activities of the parent's involvement with their children in the school. The parent advocate would go to the home and see to it that the parent reads to the child, set up an area where the child can to do homework.

The advocate would get the parent in adult education classes, if necessary, to assist the parent with reading to their children. This would demonstrate to the children that the parent values education, even after becoming an adult, because, if education is valued in the child's home, it will be valued by the child. The parent advocate would serve as a mentor for the parent in assisting the parent in whatever their needs were in educating their children. If a child can read, write, compute and speak with clarity and understanding, the child will be successful in life, because a well-read person is a well rounded and balanced person.

The parent advocate has to be a person who is compassionate, tolerant, patient and concerned about children learning to read. The advocate has to be specially selected with a personality that can gain people's confidence, trust and be willing to go into any home without being judgmental. You don't want parents to feel guilty or embarrassed by their living conditions, station in life, poverty or if they can't read or write themselves. The main objective of the paid parent advocate is to make it possible for every child to be able to read, regardless of what the child's status is in life or living environment.

The advocate would give a monthly, written report to the parent, the school, PTA, PTO, the school principal, the parent's employer, if she/he works. The parent advocate would be under the supervision of the school principal. The school would provide the necessary resources to the parent advocate to accommodate the parent and the child. The advocate would secure from the principal a list of those students who are failing; not learning to read and not passing the state required tests. From this list, the parent advocate would start with the most at-risk child and go to the home to find out why the parent is not involved in the child's education. Whatever barriers, excuses or problems are preventing the parent from participating in the child's learning, the advocate would resolve them, by any means necessary (within the law, of course). For example, the parent advocate would consult with the parent's employer for leave time for that parent. The employer would benefit by counting the parent's volunteer hours as the employer's contribution supporting the school system and the community. With this approach, everybody wins. The number of at-risk children who learned to read and/or met the state standards in reading would be the criteria for evaluation.

Today in our educational system in order for schools and teachers to be effective in educating children today, there must be a working relationship and partnership with parents.

Today parents are becoming more vocal about being involved in the educational decision-making for their children. Arnold F. Fege's article in Educational Leadership, titled <u>From Fun Raising to Hell Raising: New Roles for Parents</u>, wrote:

PARENTS AS PARTNERS

The current structure of public schooling does not invite public engagement, but instead reinforces a hierarchical and bureaucratic pattern that gives neither the students nor parents an official voice. Instead of opening up and encouraging genuine parental participation, the school structure eliminates anything that might erode the power equilibrium. Schools too often shut parents out of decision making and offer only limited participation, such as fundraising and volunteering.

However, today's parents are vocal and demanding in their relations with the school. They question school authority and instructional decisions. More and more, they see themselves as purchasers of public education with a right to demand from schools individualized services. For example, to express their views about, and have a more direct impact on issues that affect them, a growing number of parents have adopted a form of direct democracy that goes beyond unresponsive school boards and traditional representational decision making: Internet networking and the Federal Government (Fege 2000 ¶ 1-3).

PARENTS TO KIDS PROGRAMS/WORKSHOPS

This is another way to involve parents in the education of their children at school. This is a Title I sponsored program paid for by the Federal Government. It involves two hours a week for seven weeks where parents and children work together with teachers. Parents and children are separated the first hour. The teachers work with the children on an activity in which they will produce a product at the end of the session. The product could be a picture that they have painted, a story that they have written, or something they made with clay or other materials.

The parents are being instructed by another teacher in a different area away from the children. Parents learn how to work with their children at home on oral language development and various pre-reading and reading skills. They are also required to keep a written journal of each session.

The second hour, the parents and children are reunited. The parents practiced one of the learned skills with their children based on the same topic that the children were working on in their own session. The teachers act as "coaches" in assisting parents, giving suggestions, and making comments. Then the parents and child are given a home activity to practice before the next session. At the end of the program, parents are given a crate of supplies and materials to work with their children at home on the skills they have learned during the program/workshop.

The ultimate intent and focus of this program/workshop is assisting parents to help their children become good readers. Because the more you read, the better you read. If a child can read well, a child will continue to read and read voluntarily and independently. Reading is fundamental to everything in life.

Fege further elaborated on the new role of parents as stated below:

FAMILIES AS EDUCATORS

Although schools have resisted change, the family has restructured. The result: 21st century families attempting to partner with 20th century school organizations. The institutions of families and schools are crashing into each other, which leads to conflict and instability in school systems.

Many parents say that the time demands of work limit their involvement in their child's education and that schools do not accommodate them by offering week night and weekend volunteer opportunities, child care, and transportation. To be sure, many parents still prefer the traditional activities that are based on trust, intimacy, and a collective responsibility for all children and consider fund raising, parent-teacher conferences, and advocating for school funding to be their civic responsibilities.

Results oriented curriculum with accountability for learning means that parents become a strategic instructional resource not only for students but also for schools, teachers, and principals, whose performance is closely scrutinized. In fact, parents become an integral part of the curriculum. The family makes essential contributions to student achievement, from earliest childhood through high school. Efforts to improve children's academic outcomes are more effective if they encompass families.

The pressure to increase academic achievement has created an interdependent relationship between parents and school leaders. Parents expect schools to achieve academic results, schools need parent involvement to do so, and parents need schools to teach their children.

Under current school structure, the teacher, principal, librarian, counselor, secretary, and support help have legal places, but parents have no guaranteed place. Many parents search for their roles and their rightful place in a structure that recognizes the importance of the professionals, but not the family. To get serious about parental involvement, every school district needs to hold school administrators accountable for involving parents, each school should develop parental engagement plans in concert with school staff and parents, and the district should help teachers who are seeking the involvement of parents. Schools must move away from a bureaucratic model and place the needs of students and families at the apex of school response.

THE MARKET

Driven by outcomes and results, today's parents often view schools in contractual terms (charter schools, contracted learning, parental choice) and often see their interaction with the school as a marketplace relationship based on commerce and transactions, not as a social responsibility driven by civic and democratic duty. Without the civic dimension, the common school ceases to be a formal institutional voice for public participation, and public schools become nothing more than vehicles to satisfy private interests. But in an age of increasing educational competition, public schools and school districts need to communicate to parents and the community the answer to this question: Why should I send my child to a public school?

Educators have not viewed parents and the community as a market. As a result, parental and community involvement have often played secondary roles in the framework of public education, especially in poor and disadvantaged school districts. Instead of developing a market-sensitive structure, educators reinforce traditional power dynamics. They are unwilling to redistribute their prerogatives.

Decisions about parental needs, courteous service, teacher-parent relationships, staff recruitment, effective and frequent communications, teacher competency, and parental attitudes will rise to prominence as important management priorities. Families will evaluate schools on the basis of how responsive they are to their needs. Thus, the scope of school management should encompass more comprehensively the entire education and instructional process.

Being more responsive to parents and the community market, however, does not mean that the school district must abandon the virtue of the common good or resort to privatization, school vouchers, or charters. A November 1999 national poll conducted by Peter D. Hart Research Associates for the Public Education Network and authored by Wendy D. Puriefoy, President, Public Education Network, "All for All: Strengthening Community Involvement for All Students," demonstrated an overwhelming national commitment to public schools. A vast majority of respondents (89%) identified schools that provide a quality education as a "very important" community priority. They also favored bolstering community involvement (85%) over introducing vouchers. Over 70 percent of the respondents also believed that involving individuals in meeting community needs and solving community problems is very important. These results suggest that a large market understands the importance of public education and prefers not to abandon the public schools.

The poll also demonstrates that parents feel excluded from, or without a role in, their local school. Although schools believe that community involvement is essential for school improvement, they are frequently unprepared to take advantage of this willingness to participate in meaningful school activities. Whereas 47 percent of those polled said that time was a barrier to participation, 48 percent said that they were not given the opportunity to become involved, did not know how to, or felt that their individual involvement did not make a difference. This large market of untapped support for public education will eventually be targeted by private, contracted, or religious schools.

Schools should make a special effort to reach absent parents. The customer who does not become involved is as important as the customer who does. In many cases, the uninvolved parent is the person with whom we should start to communicate about innovations and changes. Is that customer:

- Dissatisfied?
- Shopping elsewhere?
- Spreading bad or untruthful information about the school?
- Intimidated by school staff?
- Unable to read or understand the school's communications?
- Misunderstanding his or her importance to the academic success of the child?
- Affected by a school schedule that is not compatible with the family schedule?
- Discouraged from engaging in school activities?
- Never asked to become involved?
- Made to feel unwelcome.
- Not appreciated.

Schools can no longer characterize the uninvolved parent as apathetic. Purposeful outreach and marketing strategies are needed to communicate with all parents the assets and importance of the public schools (Fege 2000 ¶ 8-19).

Educators have conducted numerous studies on the role of parents in rearing children. In my opinion, the most profound statements that have been made in the educational arena were made by The National Education Association. There were six National Educational goals based upon these studies in 1994. They are as follows:

Goal 1: By the year 2000, all children in America will start school ready to learn.

Goal 2: By the year 2000, their high school graduation rate will increase to at least 90 percent.

Goal 3: By the year 2000, American students will leave grades 4, 8, and 12 having demonstrated competency in challenging subject matter including English, mathematics, science, history, and geography, and every school in America will ensure that all students learn to use their minds well. So they may be prepared for responsible citizenship, further learning, and productive employment in our economy.

Goal 4: By the year 2000, U.S. students will be first in the world in mathematics and science achievement.

Goal 5: By the year 2000, every adult American will be literate and will possess the skills necessary to complete in a global economy and exercise the rights and responsibilities of citizenship.

Goal 6: By the year 2000, every school in America will be free of drugs and violence and will offer a disciplined environment conducive to learning.

As of today, we have failed every goal. So, you can see, parents, grandparents, responsible adult family members, volunteers, good citizens and good teachers and administrators, we have many, many challenges, and they are our responsibilities. Again, I would like to point out that you don't have to be rich or even have completed high school, as a parent, you just need to have the desire and the will to assist your children in succeeding in life. My mother, who completed the 3rd grade and my father who didn't attend school at all, and who was not in my home, knew how important a good education was for me. If education is valued in the home, it will be valued by the child.

COLLECTIVE NEEDS AND CIVIC RESPONSIBILITY

Arnold F. Fege, as President of Public Advocacy for Kids, made the following view points: The competing tensions between market-driven behavior and the collective needs of the public in ensuring a quality education for all children obligate education leaders to balance the needs of the citizen and the demands of the customer. Collective involvement and individual efforts can work in tandem only in the presence of a strong and widely held parental and community vision about public education. Without that connectedness and ownership of purpose, we will create a system that defines parental involvement as contracting exactly as each parent wishes, meeting individual needs as each parent sees fit, and having parents listen only to information and ideas with which they are comfortable. No one will worry about the civic aspects of participation because parents may never come in contact with one another. They can chose to come to the table or not, or, as in home schooling, they can be on their own.

This is the institutional dilemma: How do schools become more responsive to individual, market-based tendencies of parents and the community, while creating a passion and a zeal for the common good? Schools must understand the deep differences between the democratic and the market conceptions, but they have no models--or even language to help the two sides talk with each other when opposition, differences, or controversy threaten to divide camps. In many cases, the school is at a disadvantage in coping with either camp. Schools have not opened up their structures to allow genuine democratic conversations or engagement and certainly are not prepared to cope with highly individualistic, market-driven parental demands.

THE CHALLENGE OF ACCOUNTABILITY

Nowhere is this conflicting system of institutional values more evident than in the current emphasis on standards and assessments. Ten years ago, at a national education summit, governors committed states to improving their educational systems, providing educational opportunities for all children, closing the educational achievement gap between disadvantaged students and others, and increasing student achievement levels.

At that point, government leaders lost a defining opportunity to build a civic "contract" that would hold themselves and the U.S. public accountable for achieving the goals. Using modern communications technology, such as community cable, teleconferencing, the Internet, and town meetings, they could have mobilized the people in seeking answers to fundamental collective questions necessary to promote the common good. What knowledge, values, skills, and sensibilities should public schools nurture in children? What must the nation commit to in reaching the goals? What kind of work and resources must parents, teachers, students, businesses, and the community commit to? What policies and practices need to change? Above all, what is the nature of support that the community must provide for its schools to successfully implement the new American dream for its children and youth?

This effort would have promoted a two-way conversation cutting across cultural, racial, ethnic, and language differences and raising awareness about everyone's commitment to children who need special help. The eminent education historian Lawrence Cremin called this kind of debate the "genius of American education." He said that public debate educates and that education will affect the entire apparatus by which the public itself is created and renewed.

Instead, leaders responded to the cry for high academic expectations by installing standards and high-stakes testing without either going to the people or testing the market. Technocrats -- psychometricians and statisticians conducted most of the standards work outside public view. Little public debate occurred until the standards and high-stakes assessments were rolled out. These highly technical, abstract, and esoteric standards and assessments silenced a public discussion of alternative ways to reform the public schools. However, the public backlash created by the standards confusion is unifying market behavior and democratic behavior, both the parents who are concerned about the impact of standards on their own children and the citizens who are concerned about the impact on the collective future of public education.

Educational improvement needs more than parental involvement. It also needs to rally the community around a common vision and purpose. Parental involvement has become the substitute for an entire community's organizing in support of its public schools. Without a public behind us, without parental ownership of its schools, and without a clear and articulate vision about what binds parents and the community of all colors, races, and languages in a common purpose, individualism will render obsolete our hope that all children receive a quality public education (Fege 2000, ¶ 20-26).

Parade Magazine, May 16, 1993 issue, written by Mark Clements conducted an extensive survey and research study titled "What's wrong with our schools."

- 63% of Americans rate the quality of public education as poor or fair.
- 79% think there should be a moment of silence during school when children can pray if they want to.
- 88% say schools should teach sex education.
- 77% say parents should have some influence in choosing the books that students read.

Are our public schools making the grade? Almost two-thirds (63%) of Americans rate the quality of public education as poor or fair at best. In fact, 60% of all those questioned (71% of blacks and Hispanics) say they would pay more taxes if the money went to the public schools in their communities.

These findings are based on an exclusive PARADE survey of 2,512 men and women, aged 18 to 75 and representative of the nation as a whole. "What impresses me the most is that people not only want more government support for education, but they're also willing to pay more from their own pockets, says Sava, executive director of the National Association of Elementary School Principals. Poverty has increased tremendously in the last decade, and more parents see that education is the only chance their children have.

Among the survey's findings:
- 79% say there should be a moment of silence during school when children can pray if they want to.
- 62% believe that parents should be allowed to teach their children at home if they follow the required curriculum.
- 55% say that schools place too much emphasis on sports.

- 51% feel that television is a detriment to education; 35% see TV as an asset.
- 46% support extending the school year to 11 or 12 months.
- 35% say that parents who send their children to private or parochial schools should get a tax allowance.
- Only 5% rate the U.S. education system as better than Japan's or Germany's.

And, the survey suggests, we want schools to deal with the issues of times:

- 98% say that schools should teach students about drugs and their effects.
- 88% are in favor of sex education.
- 67% say schools should teach "awareness and understanding" of different religions, while 57% support similar instruction about homosexuality.

All the social problems surrounding children come with them to school every day and ultimately have an impact on their ability to learn, says Pat Henry, president of the National Parents and Teachers Association. "The public realizes that schools have to deal with these issues."

What's right-and wrong-with our schools? Only 37% of those surveyed rate the schools as good or excellent. Less that half (49%) give them high marks for teaching basic skills, and 60% say the schools do only a fair or poor job of encouraging creative thinking and curiosity. More than half, however, rate as excellent or good the special programs for the gifted (57%) and special-needs classes such as art and gym (55%).

In general, teachers get better report cards than the schools: 52% say the quality of teaching is good; 35% say it's fair. "They are trying very, very hard, but teachers can't do their jobs, because they don't get the financial resources or the moral support they need from parents" says Jeff Whisenant, 34, of Claremont, North Carolina, a laid-off clerk who has since returned to college. "A lot of teachers aren't getting paid what they deserve."

One of two respondents (50%) says teachers' salaries are "too low," 37% say they're just right, and 13% say "too high." Among the 63% who rate America's public schools as fair or poor, 13% say the basics: reading, writing and mathematics need more emphasis, while 10% agree with the statement "children graduate practically illiterate."

Randy White, 49, Donaldsonville, Georgia, taught briefly at an inner-city high school after retiring as a policeman. "Maybe I was naïve, even after twenty-five years of police work," says White, now an investigator. There were kids that could not write a paragraph. Educational standards have definitely been lowered to accommodate those who don't want to learn and have no desire to succeed."

The school environment was rated as fair or poor by 74% of respondents. "Most of my friends who were teachers have quit," says Donna Wray, 45, of Darby, Pennsylvania, who handles employee benefits for an accounting firm. "Schools have turned into giant baby-sitting classes. If they had more discipline in classrooms, students who want to would be able to learn."

Having children of different cultural backgrounds in the same class has a positive effect on education, say 55%. But if the children do not speak English, the impact is negative, say 59%. Opinion on having students with different levels of skills in the same class is mixed: 42% say the effect is positive, 36% say negative.

Beyond the three R's: Most of the nation, the survey suggests, strongly supports drug and sex education. "If schools don't take it on, kids are going to learn on the streets and get it wrong," says Randy White. "At least in school they can get the facts from people with professional training."

"Support for sex education has changed drastically in the last 20 years," says PTA President Pat Henry. "Back then, parents said, "No, it's my job. I don't want schools teaching my kids about sex." But now the problems have become so traumatic that parents realize that teaching about sex, about drugs, about AIDS prevention has to be a shared responsibility." Still 64% say that parents should be able to have youngsters excused from sex-education classes.

"Asked if condoms should be available in high schools to stop the spread of AIDS, 57% of respondents said "yes." Support for condoms in the schools is highest among Blacks and Hispanics (70%) and those aged 18 to 34 (67%). "Kids are going to do what they want anyway, so please let them be safe," says Donna Wray.

Schools do only a fair or poor job of teaching the cultural heritages of their students, say 63% of those surveyed. Among Black and Hispanic respondents, 82% give low ratings to the schools' instruction in cultural diversity. "Students who are not exposed to other cultures grow up with preconceived notions about what other people are like," says Jeff Whisenant. "They should learn about others-if only to prevent bias later in life."

What would improve our schools? "More communication with parents," say 76%. Samuel Sava, speaking on behalf of the nation's school principals, agrees: "There is no way we can educate America's children without the help of parents. The schools need to do everything possible to make sure the parents stay involved, whether that means providing after-school study centers or scheduling parent-teacher conferences on Saturdays."

Parents, respondents say, should have a "great deal of influence" over the use of school funds (47%), the curriculum (44%) and selecting and hiring administrators (36%). Parents also should have influence ("some" influence, say 53% "a great deal, " say 24% in selecting books and other instructional materials.

"Parents are the key," says Louise Mason. "They're going to have to contribute more both financially and as volunteers. In my granddaughter's class, mothers come in and work with slow readers. That's what can make a difference."

Other factors cited by respondents to improve education: better qualified teachers (75%), a safer environment for students (74%), more discipline (73%), more individual attention for students (71%), better qualified administrators (67%, better drug education (63%), smaller class size (61%), better sex education (55%) and a broader curriculum (51%).

What about government? The federal government spends too little on schools say 67%. "Government should have a stake in education," says Jeff Whisenant, "because, if society doesn't motivate youngsters to get their diploma, if it doesn't give them skills, they end up on the other side of the bench, either in the courts or on the welfare system. Education is the only way we can produce individuals who can contribute, and give as well as take" (Clements, p. 4-5).

My personal experience of observing progress in a poor and failing school was while serving as a mentor at Bonner Elementary School from 2001-2003, in Daytona Beach, Florida. A 92% Black student population with more than 94% of its students on reduced and/ or assisted federal lunch program. In 1999, the school was rated as a "failing school" (F). As a result of additional instructional resources, committed and concerned teachers, caring parents, grandparents, administrators, PTO, School Advisory Council, and an extensive mentoring program, by contrast, in 2003, Bonner Elementary School improved to an "A" school rating. This was a true demonstration of what a team approach can do in assisting parents and the school in helping children to succeed.

In our efforts to support public schools, we need to discuss educational reform. School systems are in desperate need of change in order to be productive for students. One way of accomplishing this educational reform is through parents, teachers, schools, and community working together in a community partnership, just as the author mentioned about his experiences in working with a "failing" school in Daytona Beach, Florida. Educational reform is necessary if we are going to properly educate students in public schools.

Arnold Fege stated further as President of Public Advocacy for Kids in his continued support for educational reform offered the following suggestions:

HOW TO BUILD SUPPORT FOR EDUCATIONAL REFORM

- Design a parent and community involvement plan to create a closer relationship between school and home.

- Know your community and markets. Systematically collect data about community perceptions, demographic information, sources of the community's information about schools, parental and community attitudes, and solutions to problems.

- Use issue surveys, community studies, focus groups, and polls to collect information. Also use the Internet to market public education.

- Develop a focused message about the public schools that is consistent, based on marketing data and community information, and explains why a quality public education system is important to the community.

- As a substitute for formal data collection, ask district officials to call 10 to 25 randomly selected community members. These calls not only provide information, but also give parents unexpected access to school leaders.

- Analyze how different groups of community members receive information about the schools. Parents may receive their primary information from their children's teachers; non parents, from the local newspaper or the national media; seniors, from the radio.

- Give parents and other adults the opportunity to learn about instructional strategies, learning research, and changes in school restructuring necessary to raise achievement levels.

Use PTA/PTO meetings, town meetings, the Internet, cable television, radio talk shows, or the local newspaper.

- Develop a "neighborhood walk for success" in which teams of faculty, parents, and other community members go door-to-door to talk with citizens about their needs and interests in how to improve the schools.

- Target hard-to-reach families through a home visitor program that collects parents' input on issues and hand delivers information about school and district progress.

- Treat information from the field with respect and trust, and treat community complaints as opportunities for improvements, not annoyances.

- Create a parent center in each school to provide training and information, parent skill building, and a meeting place. Designate a parent coordinator to serve as a liaison.

- Suggest that the superintendent appoint a senior staff member to be an ombudsman so that community views become visible to the superintendent.

- Use community access television, talk radio, or press conferences to make the school district's views known and to keep in touch with the community.

- Provide time for staff to communicate with families and to build relationships between the school and the community.

- Include parent input in the performance evaluation of teachers and principals. Although it requires careful planning and parent training, this approach can bring the customer closer to the instructional staff.

- Accommodate parents' schedules by providing transportation and child care when hosting events at the school. Hold school events closer to where parents live, such as at a community center, a library, or a shopping mall.

- Communicate with parents and other adults in a language they can understand. Have bilingual home-school liaisons visit non-English-speaking parents to personalize school communications. Enlist interpreters on notice to assist in effective communications (Fege 2000, ¶ 27-43).

Authors James G. Dunlevy and Tia Rice Donlevy wrote an article in the International Journal of Instructional Media, titled: <u>Perspectives on Education and School Reform: Launching and School Reform Initiatives (1997).</u> From this school reform initiative, there were four major streams or perspectives: technological, psychological, ideological, and sociological.

In his 1996 Annual Report of the college, Teachers College, Columbia University President, Arthur E. Levine, discussed the wide range of school reform initiatives undertaken throughout the United States since the publication of "<u>A Nation At Risk</u>" (1983). He noted that the reform movement has taken many turns including developments in curriculum, instruction, technology, management, governance, and finance. However, after more than a decade of experimentation, "the school reform movement can be described today as being dispersed, divided, hotly contested, and consensusless" (Levine, p. 7).

We suggest that insights culled from each of the four perspectives will yield powerful results when constructing and then implementing school reform initiatives than when narrowly focused plans are put into motion. For example, programs that strive to establish higher academic standards linked to world class benchmarks (technological perspective) certainly have merit. However, if the higher standards are implemented without attention to developmentally appropriate instruction (psychological perspective), without consideration for all learners needing to meet the higher requirements (ideological perspective), and without a focus on developing students who will be citizens, not just educated workers (sociological perspective), the educational effort will be limited in scope, and weakened in educational power.

There are many school programs that now concentrate almost solely upon psychological factors in school improvement. Developing instruction geared to multiple intelligences, for example, while educationally stimulating, may result in overlooking the need for meeting rigorous academic standards. An over-emphasis on the cognitive factor also may run the risk of injuring the social dimension to schooling. Certainly, cognitive development must be considered when designing instruction and lesson plans. But to neglect to consider the impact of social structures and norms that constitute the school context, and the many social dimensions of the school experience, is to potentially limit the reach and effectiveness of reform programming.

Further, a one-dimensional focus on the individual psychological factor in schools does little to improve the lives of children outside the dominant groups. Structural problems and institutional practices that privilege certain children and marginalize others should receive a hearing in school reform plans. Schools need to help all children, not just those in the mainstream culture. Programs that exclusively anchor reform efforts to psychological and cognitive aspects of schooling miss important opportunities to improve the lives of those children outside the dominant groups.

Today, mentally oriented programs designed to assist dysfunctional thinking and behavior with emotionally disturbed young people, and norm-based programs designed to address negative behavior of troubled youths also need to incorporate understandings that value higher academic standards for these students. Many academic programs for these youngsters take place in special education settings where there is little, if any, expectation that these children can achieve high academic standards. Such programs do a disservice to children by ignoring the power of high expectations and demanding coursework.

Additionally, school reform and improvement plans should address the pressing need of many students and families for social and medical services. Implementing rigorous academic standards at school without considering the broader needs of the family, as a whole, burdens reform initiatives with shortsightedness. Working thoughtfully with multiple community service providers to support families and children at the school site offers the possibility that educational reform might embrace and address the deeper needs of the community.

Beyond the provision of a range of services to children and families, school reform plans should include genuine questioning about the curriculum and its constitution. Engendering a sense of caring for the community and the environment offers an alternative to precision tooling of standards and their mastery as the goal of formal schooling. There are many developments in curriculum today that strive to broaden understandings of children beyond a concern with technical expertise. Connections and relationships are at the core of these developments that serve to enhance community life.

Constructing and implementing school reform plans should be guided by tension and balance among the four perspectives. High standards, competent future workers, developmentally appropriate instruction are just a few of the school reform issues that need to be addressed. Others are the nurturing of individual potential, accelerated learning for at-risk children, and a curricular celebration of the rich contributions of all cultural groups. We could also include the development of citizens, not simply workers; attending to the social and medical needs of children and families, nurturing personal character and a sense of civic duty. No school reform plan could be complete without the inclusion of enhancing social sensitivity and building a caring local and world community.

If a reform program focuses solely on one of these areas and excludes contributions from the other perspectives, the tension and balance will be lost and the reform effort will be weakened. We suggest that by maintaining a certain degree of tension and balance among the insights and contributions found within the four perspectives, school improvement plans will rest on the most secure foundation.

The technological, psychological, ideological, and sociological perspectives presented have offered a template for considering reform initiatives from a broad point of view, one that includes conflicting theoretical and practical positions. While there often appears to be a mixture of voices urging narrow agendas in the educational literature, it is the contention that the perspectives described in the school reform perspectives offer a way to bring coherence to the many divergent proposals for improving our nation's schools (Donlevy, Donlevy 1997 ¶ 1-20).

Author Mark Havens wrote an article in the School Administrator Magazine, titled <u>Beyond Money: Benefit of an Education Foundation</u>, he wrote the following comments:

> The U. S. population is aging. Households with children attending public schools are becoming an ever-smaller percentage of the U.S. population. Most school districts still function as though parents are their largest constituency.

While U.S. schools today enroll a record number of students, the number of households that do not have children in school outnumber families with school children by more than 2 to 1, and this gap is widening. Should educators and school officials be concerned about this growing differential? You bet!

Patrick Jackson, the late public relations adviser and practitioner, used to scold school officials by reminding them that the true customers of public schools are not the parents who send us their children or the businesses that employ our graduates. Rather, he would say, our key stakeholders are the taxpayers who send us their money to operate schools and who have the power to vote "yes" or "no" at the ballot box. They are the owners of our school systems.

What are American schools doing to communicate to and build relationships with these owners, especially those who don't have school-age children? One of the most powerful and effective tools schools can use to build relationships with this group is the education foundation.

While school foundations vary in their roles and activities, a school foundation is defined here as a private not-for-profit entity, usually incorporated under appropriate state laws or under the sponsorship of another private nonprofit, which is governed by a board of directors separate and distinct from the educational entity for which it was created to support.

Many, if not most, school foundations were established as fund-raising arms of the school district. Indeed, many were set up in the wake of unsuccessful efforts to pass a bond or levy measure or after a particularly nasty round of budget cuts. However, when the vision of these foundations becomes too narrow and expectations are too high, their results are often disappointing. Successful school foundations realize that their most effective role and benefits derive from goals beyond mere fund raising.

Many private and parochial elementary and secondary schools have had school foundations for decades and often rely on their fund-raising prowess to generate a large percentage of their institutional budgets. In contrast, public school foundations generally are not held responsible for providing a substantial portion of their school district's budget.

Public school foundations and local education funds had their genesis in large, urban school districts. The San Francisco Education Foundation, founded in 1979, was an early leader and model in this arena.

In 1982, the Public Education Fund, now the Public Education Network, received a grant from the Ford Foundation to assist in the creation of nearly 50 local education funds in urban and impoverished rural areas. PEN provided--and continues to provide--valuable support and guidance to its member institutions through networking, information and other resources.

In other communities, school foundations grew from local efforts entirely separate from their school district. Founders included corporate leaders, chambers of commerce, colleges and universities, other local charities, parent groups, booster clubs and alumni groups. However, the impetus for creating most foundations has arisen from school boards and school districts themselves.

No definitive count or central registry of public school foundations exists in the United States. Best estimates now put the number at well over 3,000. They operate in school districts with hundreds of thousands of students as well as districts with just a few hundred pupils. Indeed, in a few states, including Florida and Oklahoma, nearly every school district has organized a foundation.

In some locations, such as San Diego, Calif., and Pocatello, Idaho, individual schools have their own foundation, in addition to district-wide foundations. States such as West Virginia and Arizona have created statewide public school foundations to promote excellence in public schools.

School districts do not need foundations to raise money. American schools have been raising private funds for over a century through performances, product sales and other fund-raising activities. And now they also write and secure government and private grants that sometimes total millions of dollars.

So, why would a school district want or need a school foundation if it is perfectly capable of raising its own private funds? The purpose of a school foundation is no more to raise money than the purpose of a school district is to collect taxes.

The most successful school foundations use fund raising simply as a means to an end. What that end is depends on the characteristics and needs of the school district and the community it serves. School foundations are not based on a single model. Although they share some features, each foundation is unique. Foundations derive their purposes and roles from the groups that create them. These purposes and roles vary widely, and once established, they dictate most aspects of the foundation's operations. It is against these purposes that the foundation's success will be judged, so they should be clearly defined.

Some foundations define their role as an advocate for public education and school improvement. They use their resources and fund-raising abilities to be active partners in school reform campaigns, which they often initiate. They value their independence and freedom from education politics. The Public Education Network is a leader in this approach.

Many school foundations find their mission in promoting positive public relations for their schools. Foundations can be a valuable tool in a school district's communication efforts. "A foundation is, in essence, an awareness campaign," says Connie Blaney, public relations director for the Norman, Oklahoma, school district. "Our foundation serves as an advocate in the community and a partner with our schools. It is great public relations for the Norman public schools."

Dean Thornton, a retired president of the Boeing Corporation., co-founded the Seattle Alliance for Education. He echoes this sentiment from the point of view of a business leader. "Our foundation has helped improve the image of the Seattle public schools. Foundations can help with this effort in areas where the state is delinquent in its support of public education." Foundations can build bridges between schools and the public, especially community sectors that have been previously overlooked. "Foundations bring in a whole different set of patrons with whom we get to work. They find out more about our school district," says Marsha Chappelow, assistant superintendent of communication services for the Blue Valley School District in Overland Park, Kansas. "You are educating patrons as well as fund raising from them."

Communities are filled with people and organizations that don't have direct connections to schools, and yet their support is indispensable if public schools are to be successful. As parents become an ever-smaller percentage of the population and non-student households increase in number and influence, school districts must modify their public relations efforts in conjunction with this shift.

Chappelow cites senior citizens and empty nesters among the key groups that schools must reach out to. A school foundation can be a valuable player in building bridges to these targeted groups. Putting senior citizens on a foundation board is a first step in reaching out to this particular group. School foundations also have funded or operated senior volunteer programs in schools, while others have created or sponsored intergenerational programs such as "senior proms."

A school foundation in Lewiston, Idaho, launched an intergenerational cookbook project that entailed junior high students interviewing senior citizens to collect old family recipes and the history behind them. The students compiled these stories and recipes into a book, and sales of the cookbook generated three times more revenue than what it cost the foundation to produce. But it was the relationships that were created through this project that mattered most.

Other groups to target might include: public officials, retired school employees, high school alumni, and parents of preschoolers, spouses and families of school employees. In addition, single persons, ministers, real estate agents, local celebrities, small business owners, corporate officials, regional community leaders, economic development groups, civic organizations, philanthropists, foundations and higher education institutions may be targeted.

Few school districts by themselves have the resources to effectively and regularly reach out to all of these groups. And yet these groups constitute a majority of our patrons and have the potential to help or hinder the work of our schools (Havens 2001 ¶ 1-30).

Encouraging news on the education front is that many schools and school districts have progressed beyond the School Improvement Teams of the 1990's. This decentralization plan adopted by most schools districts across the U.S. has expanded. School advisory councils which include parents, schools administrators, staff members and community people from all walks of life, are now becoming more commonplace. These schools advisory councils (SAC's) become very involved in decision-making at the individual school levels. This varied group of citizens examines school's improvement plan, its strategies, test scores and budget.

Though not a policy-making committee, the SAC can recommend and advise school administrators on budget and other major decisions. This body also brings community opinions, comments and feelings to school administrators which help the teachers and principals to gauge their relationship with parents and community. This kind of interaction between parents, the school and the community can only bring an improvement in education for all children and increased cooperation for all groups involved.

The role of school from my personal experiences with assisting parents in rearing their children is "one knows the water best who has swum in it." Experience is worth more than mere theory and bare book learning. Truths digested in textbooks are not fully learned until they are brought home in actual living. Experience takes us beyond the limits of a book.

So, in the last analysis, the most learned or the most experienced, they know the ins and the outs, the ups and the downs. Where some are going, they have already been. It's the school experience that enhances the parent in rearing children.

Chapter 7

The Role of Community Volunteers and Leaders in Rearing Children

"Giving of one's time, energy, and expertise is what builds character in Children."

If we perceive the school as an integral part of the surrounding community, reflecting the social and economic issues of the neighborhood culture, then the school and the role of community volunteers assumes a very important and central role.

The history of community volunteer programs in this country is rich in its tradition. Voluntary organizations in the United States have a long-standing history of providing services and assistance to needy people. The subject of volunteering is one of growing interest as funds for human resources programs are cut back at the federal level. This makes the role of community volunteers even more important with assisting children in school.

There are numerous kinds of community volunteer programs from mentoring, tutoring, after school, child care, big brothers, big sisters, PTA's/PTO's, YMCA, to various clubs. But the key things they all have in common are building better schools, children, and communities.

The dictionary defines "volunteer" as a person who works for an institution or cause without pay, giving freely of his or her time and effort. Today, community volunteers around the country represent more than 95 million people who do everything from counseling teens to stay in school, to working with the hungry, and homeless. The first national community volunteer week observance began April 20, 1974 and was established by a presidential proclamation to focus public attention on the great contributions of our nation's volunteers.

Volunteers have the power to move mountains. They have the power to make good things happen while being innovative and creative. Like democracy, volunteering must be actively preserved and protected. It doesn't just happen. Volunteering grows out of the leadership of creatively committed people who are willing to share their time, talent, and energies with others. Its future will be shaped both by the work of these people and by the interaction of the volunteer community with the rest of society.

The positive value of volunteering crosses all political, economic, religious, and ideological perspectives. Three of these values form the basis for a value system around which people can build their lives and be productive citizens in our communities.

The first of these is caring. Simply put, volunteering is the way we say, it's "OK" to care. There's nothing strange, un-cool, or weird about it. More important, it is the way in which we translate our caring into positive, helping action. People who volunteer, care about other people and their problems and want to do something to help them. They care about the community and want to make it a better place for everyone to live.

The second value is problem-solving. Despite the words of contemporary social critics, volunteers believe that problems do have solutions, particularly at the personal and local community levels. Global solutions to global problems ultimately are the sum of such local solutions to parallel local problems. Volunteers have a positive belief in the possibility of such solution.

The third value is improvement. It is the most important of all because it says that the result of volunteering should be to increase the ability of all people to participate effectively in making those decisions that affect their own lives and the lives of their families, neighbors and communities. Self-sufficiency, not continued dependency, is the most desirable goal which volunteers strive. At the same time, it is recognized that with self-sufficiency comes the responsibility to act in the best interests of the community as a whole.

It is through values such as these that volunteering plays its most vital role in our society as a humanizing force that insures our individual liberties and the safety of our democratic community. These relationships are partners in the development of youth, parents, schools, business and community.

Age isn't a requirement to be a volunteer even though we think only retired people are volunteering their time and services. Today, there is a new breed of volunteers, young and old, male and female, black and white. Ninety-five (95) million people or 51% of Americans volunteered 22 billion hours. The value of this time in 2001 was $200 billion.

➤ The average hours volunteered per week has increased to 4.2, slightly higher than the four hours per week in 1989.

➤ Forty-eight percent of volunteers gave five or more hours per week.

➤ Fourteen percent of volunteers gave five or more hours per week.

➤ The business sector accounts for the fastest growing pool of volunteer resources. Between 1995 and 2000, the number of companies implementing volunteer programs rose from 700 to 1,000.

➤ Minority groups are asked to volunteer less often, but, when asked, volunteer at a higher rate than the average population.

➢ African Americans are volunteering in greater numbers. The number of volunteers rose from 48% in 1999 to 53% in 2001.

➢ Forty-eighty percent of single persons volunteered in 2001, up from 44% in 1999.

➢ Those who identify themselves as religious and who attend religious services regularly are by far the most generous with their volunteer time.

➢ Nearly seventy-five percent believe that charitable organizations play a major role in making communities a better place to live.

The American spirit of compassion and creativity is leading to a greater range of volunteer opportunities, according to those who study the subject. Many people are developing their own unique ways to provide service to their communities.

The fastest and most significant way to increase volunteerism is to ask more people to help. Among the 44% of respondents who were asked to volunteer in 2004, 86% actually did. Among the 55% who were not asked, only 24% volunteered. Volunteers are the only human beings on the face of the earth who reflect this nation's compassion, unselfish caring patience, and just plain love for one another.

The magnitude of our social problems will require that all citizens and institutions make a commitment to volunteering as a way of life and as a primary opportunity to create needed change. Former President John Kennedy said, *"My fellow Americans, ask not what your country can do for you, ask what you can do for your country."* Sure the world is full of trouble, but as long as we have people undoing trouble, we have a pretty good world. Volunteerism flourishes in a free society among individuals who live by the golden rule, yet see the need for self-actualization.

I believe when they volunteer, employees feel personal fulfillment. They feel good about themselves and that often translates to feeling good about the company. If you feel good about yourself, it will carry over to other people. It is when you give of yourself that you truly give. I'm often reminded of the young man who told his father that for 25 years he gave him money and material things, but he didn't give himself. Behold, I do not give lectures or a little charity, when I give, I give myself, because giving of one's self remains for a lifetime. Voluntary participation strengthens us as a nation, strengthens our schools, communities and fulfills us as individual human beings.

No act of kindness, no matter how small, is ever wasted. So, in today's competitive society where public schools aren't funded at the levels they deserve, teachers aren't being paid enough for all they do. Community volunteers are necessary in order for public schools to stay competitive, current and more viable in today's society. To the volunteers who have served so faithfully, you are an invaluable asset to the school system. You are the extra strength and glue that keeps things going, the difference between a marginal school and a great school. You are the mothers, fathers, grandmothers, grandfathers, friends, former educators and just plain, down to earth people who really care about our young people and the future of our public schools to give your precious time and service. You are special volunteers. You make life a little easier to bear in a day-to-day situation at our schools. Because of you, the schools will always be indebted to volunteers. As valuable resources to our schools/community concept, you can bring back to the community positive information and positive news about the school. You serve as ambassadors of good will for our public school. As volunteers, you truly bring good things to light. It is only proper to set aside a time once a year to acknowledge all that volunteers do for our future, schools, children and community. Think of all the young minds you can reach, and teach. They could be potential doctors, lawyers, teachers, preachers, politicians and leaders. As Dr. Martin Luther King, Jr. once said, *"Everyone can be great because everyone can serve."* Not only have you volunteered, you have volunteered consistently and faithfully.

As community volunteers and mentors, you serve as role models for children while giving of your time, energy, resources, and expertise. So, it is imperative that you lead by setting positive examples, because children will observe, retain and emulate you.

Children are a product of their environment good or bad. If we spend quality time with our children on a consistent basis, we will have less discipline problems with them. Children learn from adults, older children, their siblings, and peers. So, we as responsible adults need to be careful of what we do and say around our children at all times.

To all concerned citizens, community volunteers in our schools, bring good things to light. Community volunteers are our greatest natural resource in building better students, schools and communities. Volunteers will make better human beings and strengthen our country. More community volunteers are needed to provide mentoring for our young people in schools.

Why Mentoring?

- Teachers rate learning from other teachers as second only to their own teaching experiences as the most valuable source of information about effective teaching.

- The positive reinforcement received through coaching validates those things which teachers already do effectively.

- Coaching facilitates the creation of norms that break down isolation and promote the exchange of ideas through collaborative problem solving.

- Eighty percent of teachers who received instruction with follow-up coaching report implementing new strategies in their classrooms. Without coaching, this number drops to only ten percent.

- Teachers' skill development is markedly increased when opportunities for practice and feedback follow staff development instruction.

- Following peer coaching, teachers report substantial increases in the use of skills and strategies to support instructional change.

- Teachers who received coaching for two years improved more in their teaching skills than those that received this help for only one year.

- To be successful, coaching must be separated from contractual evaluation.

For the past four years, the author has served as a mentor at Bonner Elementary School in Daytona Beach, Florida. This is a well-structured and highly professional program for mentors. The program is titled HOST (Help One Student to Succeed). The HOST program was implemented in March 2000 after Bonner Elementary School was declared a failing school "F" by the state of Florida in 1999 on the FCAT (Florida Comprehensive Achievement Test). The Bonner Elementary HOST program is coordinated by Lannette Bertholf. The program description is listed below addressing the following questions:

Mentoring Program at Bonner Elementary School in Daytona Beach, Florida:

How long has nominee been volunteering for your organization?

Hours per month: 120. The HOST (Help One Student to Succeed) Program at Bonner Elementary, Daytona Beach, Florida was started in March 2000. Over 70 students and approximately 150 mentors participated. This translates into an average of 120 volunteer hours a month, 2,145 hours total since 2000.

Describe the outstanding volunteer activity/activities performed by the nominee.

Mentors are recruited from the community. Each mentor agrees to volunteer a minimum of thirty minutes per week; however, there are many mentors who volunteer sixty minutes or more. Each mentor works individually with the same student each week. All mentors receive initial and on-going training on the most effective reading strategies to use with their students. Each time a mentor and student meet, they read together and discuss the text they are reading. They also work together on vocabulary and fluency. The mentors keep records of their student's progress and offer encouragement and specific praise.

What was the impact of the nominee's volunteer activity upon the quality of life in the community?

The HOST mentors that volunteer at Bonner are a blend of professional people, college students, and retirees. All are outstanding and involved members of this community. Since most of Bonner's students live in poverty, these mentors enrich their students' lives by forming relationships with them.

They give the students the attention and encouragement necessary to foster self confidence. One-on-one academic mentoring builds the students' self esteem and gives them the confidence necessary to be successful. All Bonner Elementary students showed significant learning gains in reading in the course of the year.

What role did the nominee play in initiating the activity?

All of the mentors are volunteers. Many of them give up their lunch hour to come to Bonner to work with their students. These mentors recruit their friends, family, and co-workers to become mentors in the HOST program. A significant number of the mentors have been with the "HOSTS" program for more than a year.

Does the volunteer have previous volunteer experience and/or is the volunteer currently involved in other volunteer activities?

Some of the mentors have been involved in other tutoring experiences. However, many of them choose to stay in the HOSTS program because they enjoy working with the same student each week. This allows each mentor to form a bond with his/her student and to enjoy seeing the student grow and improve over time. Also, these mentors participate in fund raising activities for the HOSTS program such as the Future's Bowl-a-thon. In 2001, the mentors at Bonner Elementary school raised the most money in the county: $2,471.00! HOSTS mentors also collected food items for the school's Thanksgiving Basket Brigade, which resulted in 35 families receiving canned foods and children's books for their students. During Christmas and before summer break, the mentors donated money for books for their students.

Why do you feel this person or group deserves an outstanding volunteer award (include any interesting or unusual information about the volunteer(s).

HOSTS mentors at Bonner provide a much needed service. They work with elementary children who are deprived because of a life of poverty and turn them into successful readers. These mentors are dedicated and committed to the students with whom they work. Each mentor gives time out of their busy schedule to spend with their student. Besides giving of their time to mentor, many of these people also donate money for the program and don't miss a chance to recruit a friend or co-worker to also be a mentor. Each student who is fortunate enough to participate in the HOSTS program has not just had their reading skills enriched, but their lives as well. These mentors give the greatest gift one person can give another...they believe in their students! As a result of all the hard work, commitment, dedication, financial resources, and time the mentors gave to Bonner Elementary students, the school improved from a "failing" school with a grade of "F" to a passing grade of "A" for the 2002-2003 school year.

To all concerned citizens, there are numerous ways to get involved with community schools. Volunteering requires a little commitment and time. By investing your expertise as a volunteer, you are investing in children. Because children are our greatest resource, are extensions of us, and our future.

Get Involved In the School

Volunteering at a school or taking part in the school planning process are two exciting ways to offer your talents and communicate your concerns to the school. Working parents can get involved to the extent their time allows. Both the school and your child appreciate whatever participation you can give.

Be A Volunteer: Volunteers in Public Schools

Volunteers involve all segments of the community and all age groups, from students to seniors, who help meet the needs of our students through the enhancement of education. Volunteers help improve instruction, enrich curriculum, close the "generation gap," and improve school/community relations. Volunteers serve in almost every aspect of school education, from assisting in the classroom, school office, health room, media center, special area, and adjunct classrooms, to working with PTA/PTSA, the School Advisory Council, academic enhancement programs, and student extracurricular organizations. Each school's program is unique in response to needs determined by the school's professional educators.

Catherine C. DuCharme has done a great deal of research on improving the lives of children through education. In the Education Magazine (1998), she wrote an extensive article focusing on the work of Faye and Frank Clarke on educating and saving children. The article is as follows:

According to Faye and Frank Clarke in their article titled <u>"They're all our Children": and their Crusade to Educate The Children,"</u> wrote in 1998, everybody can do something. Even if one person reached out to a child one time, that's a contribution. If one person looks in a child's eyes expecting that that child can learn and deserves the help, that's a contribution. No matter how tiny, if every single one of us just did something. This is a crusade to save the children, to save the country, to save our future, to save our grandchildren's future and your grandchildren's future.

There is a quiet crisis in our nation. Though the United States is "the most technologically advanced, affluent, and democratic society the world has ever known, the crucially formative years of early childhood have become a time of peril and loss of millions of children and their families" (Carnegie Corporation of New York 1994, p vii).

Too many school age children are not achieving in school to their full potential as they should. The report of the Carnegie Task Force on Learning in the Primary Grades, Years of Promise, highlights the pattern of underachievement in our nation (Carnegie Corporation of New York, 1996).

The pattern of underachievement is especially stark for children of low-income families and children of diverse cultural, linguistic, and racial backgrounds, who by and large are not receiving the teaching and support they should have as they move from home to school to neighborhood and other settings in the course of the day. For them, the deck can be unfairly stacked against academic success, and the years of promise can fade to hopelessness and resignation (Carnegie Corporation of New York, 1996, p.4).

Faye and Frank Clarke are committed to ensuring that every child receives an equitable education. They have made a conscious decision to serve their community as retired citizens; they donated their time and energy to improving the lives of children. Through their work as founders of "Educate the Children Foundation," they are dedicated to "helping raise the level of learning of children in the poorest school districts in the United States of America. They do this by providing them and their teachers with tools, technology, supplies and equipment that will increase their interest, motivation and enthusiasm for learning; and will prepare them to live productively, achieve to the maximum of their ability, and contribute positively to our society" (Educate the Children Foundation, n.d.). To that end, the Clarkes provide books and equipment, furniture, computers, motivational speeches, training for teachers, and "hand holding" for teachers.

Frank Clarke states: We want teachers to see that there are some helping hands out there that are really concerned abut them and the children…if we don't educate the children much better than they're being educated now, we're going to have some serious problems with our nation after we're dead and gone. I think we have a duty and an obligation as citizens to take the responsibility for helping to improve education in general, especially in the elementary school, wherever we can, as much as we can, (Frank Clarke, personal communication, July 2, 1998).

Faye Clarke adds: Just the fact that someone outside that school district recognizes the problem and is stepping up and trying to do something is inspiration to the teachers; it's encouraging to everyone, (Faye Clarke, personal communication, July 2, 1998).

The work of Faye and Frank Clarke typifies other successful collaborative ventures in which dedicated individuals work tirelessly for the purpose of raising the achievement of children in the poorest schools (e.g., Ladson-Billings, 1994; Quint, 1994; Wolk & Rodman, 1994).

The need for action is great for too many of our nation's children who do not receive a fair start in life. Horace Mann once said, "Education is the greatest equalizer," the Clarkes agree. However, "savage inequalities" are evident in our nation's schools (Kozol, 1991). The poorest and neediest children in our country attend schools with leaky roofs, chipped paint, too few books, and an inadequate supply of educational equipment including computers (Children's Defense Fund, 1998; Kozol, 1991). The 1997 Condition of Education report found that more than 70 percent of teachers working in schools serving low-income children lacked important materials, 53 percent compared to 88 percent of more affluent schools had access to the internet, and teacher qualifications and salaries as well as per pupil spending were significantly lower in schools serving high concentrations of poor children (Children Defense Fund, 1998). The General Accounting Office reported in 1995, that "schools in central cities and those with over 50 percent minority enrollment are more likely than others to have insufficient technology and unsatisfactory environmental conditions" (Children's Defense Fund, 1998, p. 50). This is particularly alarming since a growing body or research suggests a linkage of achievement to students' physical surrounding (Children's Defense Fund, 1998). Overcrowded buildings, lack of or faulty air conditioning, and substandard facilities and equipment appear to yield lower academic performance.

If each and every child is to be afforded a fair start in life, it must begin with a sound equitable education. In order to achieve educational equity "political and civic leaders, educators, and ordinary citizens must join forces to ensure that our schools provide educational opportunities for all children, not just a privileged few" (Children's Defense Fund, 1998, p. 51), a collaborative approach is needed.

Quint (1994) highlighted the importance of a systems approach to achieving educational equity. If we perceive the school as an integral part of the surrounding community, reflecting the social and economic issues of the neighborhood culture, then the school assumes a central role. It becomes an organ of the community, with a continuous flow of ideas and people into and through it-an open system. However, if we think only in terms of students teachers, principals, administrators, and boards of education, we unwittingly create an enclosed system from which parents, doctors, social workers, businesses, and innumerable interactive agencies are barred.

Since 1991, Faye and Frank Clarke have become involved as participants in a systems approach to educating the children, our nation's future. They have targeted 100 of the most needy schools in the nation; currently they are assisting 78 schools.

More than $20 million worth of books, supplies, and equipment have been distributed to needy schools in Arkansas, Alabama, Mississippi, Louisiana, Missouri, Maryland, Washington, DC, California, Texas, and Ohio. In addition, books and supplies have been distributed in the U.S. Virgin Islands, Haiti, and Ghana, West Africa (DuCharme 1998 ¶ 1-14).

According to Jeffrey R. Young, his article in the Chronicle of Higher Education, January 31, 2003, titled "Black Students Lack Mentors in Schools," his study found the following: Black high-school students are less likely than their white classmates to form strong mentor relationships with teachers and other adult school officials--relationships that can help motivate students to attend college.

The study, an analysis of statistics from a U.S. Education Department survey that tracked 14,915 students from 1988 to 1994, found that students who formed good relationships with officials in high school had higher educational expectations and were more likely to attend college than students who lacked those relationships. It also found that black students formed those relationships less frequently than did white students.

"They're less likely than a white student to have teachers talking with students-actually forming that relationship where a teacher and student are talking," said George L. Wimberly who is a research associate at ACT Inc., which administers the ACT college-entrance examination. Exactly why the gap exists is not clear said Mr. Wimberly. "Students develop trust and respect for their teachers when their cultural identity is supported in the classroom," he wrote in a report on the study. "Conversely, social, economic, and cultural gaps between African-American students and their teachers may make it difficult for students to form cohesive relationships."

Mr. Wimberly said that a lack of school mentors for black students could be one factor leading to the difference in college attendance between black and white young people. The study found that both black and white students had planned to attend college at nearly equal levels (88 percent of black students and 89 percent of white students), but fewer black students did so (56 percent of black students compared with 67 percent of white students). Schools should do more to "connect students to adults through school based student activities-clubs, sports, things outside of the classroom, things that will get students and adults together," said Mr. Wimberly (Young, 2003).

The roles of community leaders and community volunteers are crucial in assisting parents and schools in rearing children. In addition, Parent Teacher Associations and Organization (PTA's and PTO's) played an even bigger role. Historically, African American parents were involved in working with schools in a partnership since the late 1800's. These Black parents recognized the importance of school and community working together in rearing their children. So, 1897, the first known and organized PTA was formed.

Author Christine Woyshner wrote an article titled Race, Gender, and the Early PTA: Civic Engagement and Public Education, in the Teacher's College Record, (2003), did an extensive review of the beginning history of the PTA. The historical beginning of the PTA as we know it, started in the late 1800's. In the only talk given by a black woman at the first National Congress of Mothers (NCM; 1897) titled, "The Afro-American Mother," Frances Watkins Harper implored her white audience to respect women of color and to provide for the education of the young African American women who worked as domestic servants in their homes. She remarked, "I do not ask any special favor for the colored mother.... Trample, if you will, on our bodies, but do not crush out self-respect from our souls. If you want us to act like women, treat us like women." Invited by elite white society women to represent women of her race, Harper--writer, clubwoman, and abolitionist -- spoke from a perspective of accommodation as she appealed to NCM leaders and addressed the importance of education for African American women to the standing-room-only crowd.

Furthermore, the NCM gathering was notable because, during one of the most racist decades in American history, its organizers proclaimed that they would not draw the color line. Such was the reason for Harper's invitation, and in successive years other prominent black scholars and educators spoke at annual meetings, such as Mary Church Terrell and W. E. B. DuBois. These two positions--motherhood as woman's highest calling and racial inclusivity--were complementary ideas to the NCM. The maternalist ideology of the NCM held that motherhood was woman's most important role and that with mothering came a decidedly public obligation. Moreover, as Molly Ladd-Taylor argues, maternalist thinking necessarily transcended the racial divide.

The National Congress of Mothers is known today by the name it took on in 1924, the National Congress of Parents and Teachers, or PTA. While scholars have explored the history of civic engagement and social welfare reform through this longstanding voluntary association, to date few have examined its history in public education. William W. Cutler's recent book, Parents and Schools, is a notable exception that considers the PTA as central among a constellation of efforts to forge a working relationship between home and school, parent and teacher. Therefore, the parent-teacher movement was as much initiated by black educators and parents, but this history is obscured because African Americans wanted to work within their own organizations, beyond the reaches of white control.

Black parent-teacher associations and school improvement societies, which had begun to be organized in the 1890s, remained a local endeavor into the 1920s. With the rise of the white PTA, what had once been unacceptable for black leaders--uniting with white women in educational affairs--became a welcome opportunity to ally with a growing national organization. Seeing a strong association and potential advocate in national educational reform measures, black leaders sought a means for indirect power through an affiliation with the national PTA. However, the membership of the black PTA, or National Congress of Colored Parents and Teachers, never equaled the larger proportions of the white PTA, though it enjoyed a respectable following within the black community and national exposure through its alliance with the white PTA.

The present-day implications speak to long-held assumptions about the role of organized parents in public education and the motives of lay associations that become involved in the day-to-day administration of the schools. Today, few would question the notion that relationships between parents and teachers play a critical role in students' educational success. Such discussions are just as fervent today--in the research literature and in schools--as they were in the early twentieth century. Yet, arguably, educational professionals and volunteers have not always agreed on the best way to join forces without a power struggle. For some, parents and teachers have worked together toward similar goals but for very different reasons, while for others, parents and teachers have been at odds with each other as they worked toward the same goal (Woyshner, ¶ 1-6).

Ask community volunteers, "it is more blessed to give than to receive." The most precious gift is oneself. When you give of yourself, the giving of material things becomes a matter of the heart, an act of love, not a slavish or ritualistic act prompted solely by a sense of duty.

Giving of one's time and expertise however, is no easy task. If it enslaves the recipient, it does more harm than good. So, while we give, mentor and volunteer to the children, let's also raise them to a point where they won't be dependent, for independence is a cherished state.

Chapter 8

The Role of Local and State Government in Rearing Children

"Well rounded and well educated children are an indication of the commitment of local and state officials"

It is impossible to have local and state government without giving up some freedom, and thus the more we keep local and state government at a minimum, the more freedom we have. The best local and state governments, therefore, are the ones that give the people the broadest opportunities to work out their destiny and attain happiness.

Let's demand a local and state government that treats all its citizens alike and one that is free of dishonesty, unfairness, favoritism, selfishness, dirty politics, and short range thinking that considers only what's appealing at the moment. May we not sell our birthright to the highest bidder who buys votes with tax money.

Local and state governments have an important role in reassuring that all of our children have an equal opportunity to learn and no child will be left behind. If local citizens of a nation have too much greed on one hand and too little dedication on the other to govern themselves, they will face government by others. As a result, our children will suffer.

This chapter will address concerns citizens have with local and state government and will provide some suggestions and recommendations for change in order to assist children at home and in school. After all, we elected these state and local officials, therefore we should hold them accountable in helping us to provide resources to assist in rearing and educating children.

When we examine the American public educational scene at the present time, we find that many dedicated local and state educators have given up on the possibility of the public schools being able to provide meaningful educational experiences for all children enrolled. However, not all children are failing academically in the public schools and there are some educators who have managed to find a hospitable atmosphere for applying their skills.

Over the last two decades, many local public school officials have found it increasingly difficult to finance adequate and effective elementary and secondary schooling. Before the 1960's, many local and state school districts looked on financial assistance from the federal government as non-essential to the provisioning of adequate public schooling for the state and local areas. In the mid-1979's, 1980's, and 1990's with the increased cost of providing educational services, federal funds often times make the difference between an adequate and inadequate program of study. Some state and local school districts have come to depend on federal support for salaries and materials which were previously supplied by state and local appropriations. The federal government in the past through various special programs such as Head Start, Get Set, ESAA Title VII grants, equal opportunity grants, and many others, funneled into the state and local school districts funds that allowed local and state school districts to improve the quality of educational services for children. We now have the No Child Left Behind Federal Act of 2001, Title I, for improving the academic achievement of the disadvantaged. This 2001 Federal Act is supposed to assist state and local school districts with leveling the educational playing field for blacks, disadvantaged, and poor children in school.

One of the basic assumptions underlying American public elementary and secondary schooling is that students will learn basic literacy and other essential skills for functioning as an adult in American society during the twelve years of public schooling. But for many American children, this basic assumption has proven false. This is why state and local support is so important in assisting parents in rearing their children, to be sure that no child is left behind in school.

An article written by Gary Ratner, in the February 3, 2003 The Daytona Beach, Florida News-Journal, titled "States must be given a road map to assure no child will be lost," he noted the following: When the No Child Left Behind Act of 2001 became law a year ago with the important goal of raising all children to academic proficiency in challenging subjects, the public may have believed that finally there was a complete road map for dramatically improving public schooling. But recent experience reveals the opposite.

The chasm between the law's goal and current pupil achievement is huge. Among the 8 million black and 7 million Latino pupils nationwide, about 90 percent are below "proficient," or grade level, in reading and math. About 8 million poor pupils (50 percent) lack even "basic" or rudimentary skills at their respective grade levels.

The act essentially mandates that states receiving federal Title I funds test pupils annually and publish results. It offers limited transfers and tutoring. The law also trains teachers to meet state certification requirements, certifies all teachers as "highly qualified" by the end of the 2005-2006 school year, and annually improves learning so all pupils are academically proficient by 2014.

But it does not advise states how to change their educational systems to profoundly improve learning for the majority of public school pupils, especially the poor and racial minorities. As Judith Rizzo, former deputy chancellor for New York City's schools, recently stated: "If you don't know how to get it to the classroom level, (the law) is a waste of money."

Governors such as Jennifer Granholm of Michigan have exactly that concern. She doesn't know what Michigan should do to improve achievement, and the law does not help her. Gov. Bill Richardson of New Mexico is worried that his state's rural schools will not be able to meet the federal standards. Ignorant of what to do differently and fearful of having to disclose publicly that a large percentage of their schools are failing to educate youngsters to grade level, states have already begun to seriously weaken their criteria for what constitutes academic proficiency.

Louisiana will now deem pupils "proficient" under the law even when their achievement is actually only at the state's "basic" level. Colorado will label its pupils "proficient" even when they only achieve at the "partially proficient level." Connecticut will call its pupils "proficient" under the law even when they fail to meet the state's own reading and math performance goals. Experts expect other states will follow suit. Experience reveals that the law's purpose is already being turned upside-down.

The law was intended to induce states to figure out what changes would be required to raise virtually all pupils to academic proficiency and to institute those changes. Instead, the states, not knowing how to comply, have begun to nullify the act by deeming its goal of academic proficiency to be met by whatever level of learning they provide with business as usual.

The states, by their actions and words, are in effect, pleading with the federal government to give them a blueprint for how they can dramatically enhance schooling. To enable the states to institute the necessary fundamental changes and avoid their self-protective evisceration of the law's purpose, President Bush and Congress need to honor the plea.

Experienced educators know what the road map needs to include: For existing teachers, intensive training in subject matter; individualized mentoring in teaching skills; regular, scheduled preparation time with colleagues; and refocusing traditional professional development workshops onto meeting participants' immediate teaching needs. For new teachers, supplanting widespread 10 to 12 week education college student teaching programs with at a least 30-week, academically integrated and closely supervised field placement so all candidates are competent to teach upon graduation.

For principals and superintendents, intensive case study and experiential post-graduate programs in how to lead their teachers, parents and communities to vastly raise their expectation and pupils' learning; financial and mentoring incentives to recruit and retain only academically skilled teachers and administrators, especially for poor urban and rural areas; and replacing with capable personnel all teachers and administrators unable or unwilling, after training, to perform effectively. Federal comprehensive literacy and other public or private programs, including adult education and parenting skills, should be offered to all needy families so they can motivate and assist their children to learn, and should include surrogate mentors and tutors where necessary.

Only the federal government has the authority to lead states to adopt this road map and the capacity to fund its implementation nationwide. The government's publication of such a road map is essential to prevent leaving millions of children behind (Ratner 2003).

Former U.S. Secretary of Education, Rod Paige, made the following statement, "Every child can learn, and we mean it, and we want to act on it." He further elaborated on the following: The Facts: Raising Achievement for African Americans. The Challenge: The achievement gap is the difference among the academic performance of different ethnic groups. Even though schools are now desegregated, public education has failed to deliver the promise of quality education to African Americans.

The Solution: Attack the soft bigotry of low expectations and demand that schools close the achievement gap among minority and white students. No Child Left Behind is an unprecedented commitment and focuses not on money, but on results. For the first time in the history of the world, a society has said that we are going to educate every child. We will provide every American boy and girl with a quality education, regardless of ethnicity, income or background. Educating every child is the greatest moral challenge of our time. On the 2000 National Assessment of Educational Progress reading assessment, a national test that gauges states academic progress, 40% of white fourth graders scored at or above proficient level, compared to only 12 percent of their African American counterparts. In mathematics, African American achievement also lagged. Thirty-four percent of white fourth graders scored at or above proficient, and just five percent of African Americans scored as high achievers. The racial achievement gap is real, and it is not shrinking.

We must test all groups of students so we can measure the achievement gap, define and attack it with the full knowledge and support of our communities. President Bush said he is committed to eliminating the achievement gap, not hiding it within school or statewide averages. That's why he wants each school to examine achievement every year in third through eighth grades by race, ethnicity, economic background, and disabilities. That way we won't leave any group or child behind. According to Former Secretary Paige, The Department of Education is working with the National Conference of Negro Women to reach out to communities to close the achievement gap. If all the commitments that were made by President George Bush and Former Education Secretary Rod Paige are true in assisting state and local governments with educating all of our children, truly, no child will be left behind. (Paige, http://www.officialusdepartmentofeducation).

Kathryn Masterson from the Associated Press, May 2003 article in the Daytona Beach, Florida News Journal elaborated extensively on "States Fret Paying for Schools' Law. No Child Left Behind Strains Budgets." She mentioned some highlights of the No Child Left Behind Act of 2001:

- Tests will be taken in reading and mathematics by every child in grades three through eight, beginning in 2005-06. Schools must also test students in science in three grades.

- Schools must close gaps in test scores between wealthy and poor students and white and minority students.

- School districts must allow and even help students at struggling schools transfer within the district.

Also, in her article she noted that a former high school teacher from Hartford, Connecticut, Mark Boughton, was all for the intent of President Bush's sweeping education law known as the No Child Left Behind Act. Boughton is mayor of Danbury, Connecticut, a cash-strapped city of 75,000 in western Connecticut that recently eliminated 17 jobs to save money. So, when the school superintendent asked for $500,000 and 14 new employees to help implement the new law, Boughton said "no." "It's a great package, but it's useless without money behind it," said Boughton who, like Bush, is a Republican. Around the country, state and local officials are trying to figure out how they will pay for the standardized tests and other requirements of the 2001 law. Some states are even thinking about ignoring the law and forgoing federal funding. The problem is that many states and communities are struggling with an economic downturn and budget deficits so serious that some are trimming education services, not boosting them.

The goal is to have all students proficient in math and reading by 2014. How much it will cost is the mystery. "It's impossible to put any type of fiscal impact on this," said Scott Young, an education policy expert with the National Conference of State legislatures. "There are too many variables at this point."

A handful of states, including New Jersey, North Dakota, Washington and Tennessee, have passed resolutions urging Congress and the president to fully fund federal mandates, including No Child Left Behind. A few others, including Hawaii and Utah, are considering ignoring the law and forfeiting federal education funds, New Hampshire is even considering a bill that would forbid the state from spending money to implement No Child Left Behind. Since 2003, other critical issues have been raised by states addressing serious problems with the No Child Left Behind Act.

The Education Department says the government is giving billions of dollars to states to pay for No Child Left Behind. Connecticut, for example, will receive $207.6 million for fiscal year 2003.

"I think a lot of this angst is caused by interest groups that don't want to do this," said Education Undersecretary Eugene Hickok (Masterson, May 2003).

In the March 2002, USA Today article, by Former U.S. Secretary of Education, Rod Paige made the following commentary:

Schools can't improve without the help of parents

President Bush ushered in a new era in education by signing the No Child Left Behind Act into law. The act is the most sweeping change in education policy in three decades. It gives information to parents, new resources to educators, new tools to teachers and new hope to every child.

The law requires proven methods tested by science. It also gives states new flexibility and school principals, new ways to solve old problems. Yet, all of this promise could be in danger. The unprecedented moment of bipartisan cooperation could be in vain unless we have the help of parents.

Congress passed a plan with overwhelming bipartisan support that recognizes that every parent needs the information and the options to get involved in their child's education. For schools to improve, parents must let their local schools know that they will support this law, will do their part to assist teachers and will help track their schools' improvement.

That's why parents must understand a few simple aspects of this law and the power it puts in their hands. Today, I will be embarking on a nationwide tour to at least 25 cities to provide parents with that information and to seek their active participation in this process of improving our schools.

Secretary Paige said, as a former superintendent of schools in Houston Texas, he had seen both the promise and peril of reforming schools. He had seen how bureaucracy, regulation and special interests can cripple sincere efforts to raise the quality of school districts. He had also seen in his hometown of Houston, how a few reforms, pressed forward with moral confidence and parental support, can bring the change and the hope we want for every child.

Parents, Speak Up

For No Child Left Behind to work, we need the energy, enthusiasm and expectations of parents. We need them to tell their local schools, their state officials and their elected representatives that this law doesn't just increase the resources, it also expects results. He had heard from some educators at the state level that many of their schools won't meet the standards Congress and the president have set for them. We will not lower our standards. We will redouble our efforts. Parents can play an important part in these efforts by reminding their local officials that we are all united for results and that we expect every child to learn.

The No Child Left Behind Law has four basic principles that will strengthen the education system:

1. Parents can expect schools to be accountable for the resources they are given and the results they produce.

2. They can expect schools to use solid research for instruction. Parents should know that the federal government will fund only lessons, textbooks and curricula that are proven to work by solid scientific research. That means good instruction in your child's classroom.

3. Parents should also know their schools and principals have unprecedented flexibility with federal funds. If they have a local

problem that has gone unsolved for years, they can work with their local educators to solve it by re-directing federal resources to get help where it is needed most.

4. Parents have the option, should a school fail to improve after all of these new resources and assistance have been provided, to get extra help so that their children do not fall behind. Those services range from after-school tutoring and remedial education to even transportation to another public school that is succeeding.

In turn, school officials must realize that parents understand that their schools will be held accountable, so they must improve. Officials need to see informed and interested parents looking at their state's yearly tests of reading and math. They must see that we are all united to improve the schools and look forward to the new era of No Child Left Behind.

If no child is to be left behind, it means every American must take a stand to get involved and change the culture and expectations we have for every school. And the most important help of all will be parents who care, parents who read with their children and parents who are informed so they can get their child the very best education possible (Paige, 2002)

American public education can be made to realize its potential in assisting parents with rearing their children with full support in a partnership between federal, state and local governments. Together, we have all the financial resources and educated minds, now we need the commitment to make things happen for all our children.

Chapter 9

The Role of Federal Government in Rearing Children

"Serious Quality Assurance and Compliance Insures that No Child is Left Behind in America"

The role of the federal government in assisting parents with rearing their children has a great deal to do with our government/ democracy commitment to educating all children, rich, poor, black, brown, white, male, or female. What is democracy and its purpose? "The purpose of democracy is to organize society in such a way that each member may develop his personality primarily through activities designed for the well-being of his/her fellow members and of society as a whole. Consequently, education in a democracy, both within and without school should develop in each individual the knowledge, interests, ideals, habits, and powers whereby he will find his place and use that place to shape both himself and society toward ever nobler ends."

Most educators and casual observers of the American educational scene have come to realize that there are presently serious problems facing public elementary and secondary education in the United States. Each year while the cost of providing adequate public schooling for American children and adults increases, the traditional economic and societal benefits from providing this schooling decrease. Economists of education have generally been preoccupied with calculating the economic value or benefits to the individual and the society of public elementary, secondary, and higher education. Many have concluded that with regard to elementary education in the United States, it still represents a "worthwhile investment" for the individual because of the absence of any "time-cost."

It is unlikely that most American children age 5 to 16 would be gainfully employed during these years and therefore there would be no loss to potential income for the individual. With regard to secondary and higher education, the individual must take into account loss of potential income in determining the value of each additional year of schooling, and as a result, the return on the investment is not as great as with elementary schooling. Economist Theodore Schultz in an important essay on "Education and Economic Growth" (1961) pointed out that the demands for educational services may be for the purpose of consumption, investment, or both. With respect to the consumptive value of education, the individual is interested in schooling because it may improve the "quality of life."

The traditional "liberal education" and schooling for the use of "free time" by children and adults falls into this category. When we turn to secondary education, however, we find that it is valued as both an investment, especially for lower income individuals and families and for consumption. Working age children of lower income families often remain in school in hopes that it will bring an increase in future income. Whereas in the early 1960's, when Schultz undertook his research, higher education was primarily viewed as an investment, the recent decrease in the economic value of a college degree with regard to future income has meant that for many, attending college has a wasteful value primarily and is perceived as an investment only secondarily.

Although economists of education have been able to calculate the value of elementary, secondary, and higher schooling to the individual, they have found it generally more difficult to determine its value to society. This is an extremely important issue because public educational funding agencies only have a limited amount to invest in schooling, and therefore should be concerned about obtaining the maximum return. In the case of higher education, increased public expenditures have generally brought increased productivity by the individuals receiving the schooling, and thus has generally been viewed as "a good investment" by the public. However, the recent deterioration in the economic value of a college education to the individual has led to the suggestion that the American public may be "over-investing" in higher education. Economists will, of course, continue to debate this point but at this juncture it would appear foolhardy for any public policymaker to ignore this absence of career opportunities for entrants into the labor market at the high school, college, or graduate levels. If the decision is made to cut public expenditures for higher education, then increases must be made in the availability of public service employment which would not require fourteen or sixteen years of schooling.

When we turn to public elementary and secondary education, the issues of societal benefits and gaining the maximum return on investments are usually not the subjects of investigation by economists of education. Most researchers in this area believe that the economic advantages to the society of learning to read and write, for example, are not amenable to "cost-benefit analysis." Therefore, societal values and objectives for the most part determined the amount to be expended on elementary and secondary public schooling. Moreover, since American elementary and secondary education is decentralized, the values, goals, and wealth of individuals and families in the local areas can determine the amount, type, and quality of schooling received by children in the various school districts throughout the country. This situation has resulted in great inequality in schooling between lower and upper income children, and between black and white students. In recent years, several attempts have been made by various state and federal agencies to try and reduce these inequities through increased funding of school districts with high percentages of low income, Black pupils. The results of these efforts, however, have been somewhat dubious.

Despite the lack of obvious societal benefits from expenditures for public elementary and secondary education, most educators and the general public seems to agree that the attainment of certain social goals requires the provision of elementary and secondary schooling.

Basic literacy training, socialization, citizenship, physical fitness and related objectives serve as the major justifications for continued public financial support for elementary and secondary education. At the present time, however, educational policymakers are confronted by two interrelated educational realities:

1. Many public elementary and secondary schools are failing to meet these basic educational objectives.
2. There is very little likelihood that there will be more funds available in the future to try and correct this situation.

Public elementary and secondary schooling in the United States historically has changed in response to the larger social and economic changes in American society. The early nineteenth century "common school" provided a common curriculum of the three R's and citizenship training, plus a heavy dosage of non-denominational Protestantism. The latter component made the common schools objectionable to some religious groups, especially Roman Catholics who finally decided to start their own schools at their own expense. As the country expanded and became industrialized, the labor needs of American business and industry were met by European immigrants. The increasing need for industrial workers who possessed basic literary skills and were familiar with the less complex industrial techniques and machinery led to a campaign by American industrialists and educators to change the "common curriculum" of the public schools to include industrial education. In this way children and adults destined for American industry would receive their initial exposure to industrial processes in the public elementary and secondary schools.

The introduction of industrial education into the common school curriculum signaled a major change in American public education. No longer would all children, regardless of social class background and future employment prospects, be taught the "common curriculum," but those children who by parental choice of economic necessity would very likely end up working in American factories began to receive a type of public schooling which attempted to prepare them for their place in the emerging industrial state.

Education was viewed as something elite and privileged whites in the United States were automatically granted. As a result of this practice and behavior, African Americans were forced to form their own educational institutions. From the 1800's to the 1900's, African Americans developed elementary, secondary schools and more than one hundred four-year colleges and universities in America, primarily to educate Blacks and people of color. In 2004, many of the historically and predominantly Black four-year colleges and universities are still functioning and extremely productive in spite of the attempts to integrate public education in the 1950s and 1960s. The debate is still alive and the verdict is still out about the impact of integration on public education. Research indicates that we have re-segregated public education back to the level it was prior to the 1950s.

During the same period, 1890, to 1920, the American public high school changed in response to the demands of the new industrial order. Before 1890, white public and private high schools were primarily upper middle class institutions, which prepared individuals for admission to higher education. With the increase in the demand of middle and lower middle class parents for a public high school curriculum which would meet the needs of their children who were not primarily interested in attending college, nor destined for unskilled or semiskilled factory labor, we find the emergence of the "differentiated" public high school curriculum with courses of study in business, trades, industrial processes, as well as preparation for college.

The report of the National Education Association's Commission on the Reorganization of Secondary Education 1918, also known as the Seven Cardinal Principles of Secondary Education, summarized the new aims and objectives of the public high school in the American democracy.

Among the seven cardinal principles or objectives of public secondary education were "good citizenship," "vocational excellence," "worthy use of leisure time" as well as the development of an "ethical character"(Schultz 1961, 1963, 1976).

This NEA report was significant because it highlighted the contemporary change in emphasis in American public education in general. Before 1880, equality of educational opportunity meant equal access for all to the "common curriculum" of the public elementary schools and to the college preparatory public high schools. By 1920, equality of educational opportunity had come to mean equal opportunity for each citizen to choose the type of public school curriculum that will allow them to find their place in the modern democratic, industrial state. Thus the changes in the larger society, i.e. the rise of the urban industrial nation, brought changes in American public elementary and secondary schooling and a reconceptualization of the traditional social goal of equality of educational opportunity.

After 1920, public elementary and secondary education continued to react and respond to the fluctuations in the social, economic, and even political trends in the larger society, but it was actually the institutions of higher education that were training those persons who contributed greatest to the increased productivity and technological advancements in the United States. Whereas the great emphasis placed on elementary, secondary, and industrial education coincided with the rise of the American industrial state. The post-industrial state of the second half of the twentieth century required the advanced training of scientists, technicians, and clerical workers in institutions of higher education. Before the 1930's, a high school education was often an important prerequisite for white-collar employment.

In the 1970's, a high school diploma did not even guarantee that the "graduate" knew how to read and write. The demands of the larger society for more highly trained college-educated workers greatly affected public elementary and secondary schooling and signaled the creation of the "lockstep" character of American public education. Eventually, the elementary school curriculum became "locked in step" with the high school courses of study that, in turn, came to reflect the requirements for admission to post-secondary institutions. This change in focus very likely had an effect upon the educational process. Thus, when an elementary school pupil asked why this specific skill or that bit of information should be learned and understood, the instructor's easiest reply would be to inform the student that it would be useful in high school or college. The "lockstep" flourished because it provided easy justification for questionable pedagogical and administrative practices, and many public school teachers refused to be held accountable for achievement in even the basic literacy skills of pupils under their tutelage for only one grade.

The lockstep character of American public schooling has contributed to the deterioration in other areas of elementary and secondary education. The average low-income student will not be motivated to achieve in elementary and secondary school if the likelihood of attending college appears remote. Middle class, college bound pupils view the elementary and secondary years as the time one spends in school before school becomes significant to one's future plans and career goals. "Elementary education" thus becomes the time spent in school between ages six and thirteen, and "secondary education" became the time adolescents spend in school. It is now "higher education" which is considered by many to be "education for life." This situation helps account for the recent drop in the average scores on the Scholastic Aptitude Tests (SAT). Lower income students who take the test are often not apprised of the significance of the examination, but even if they were, it would not necessarily motivate them to try and do better since they are able to observe many individuals in their communities who attended college, but are without employment.

Middle and upper income students who can afford college realize that they can get into the college of their choice (or a reasonable facsimile) without high score on the SAT tests and thus do not put forth any great effort to prepare for them. The lack of motivation for academic achievement in elementary and secondary school pupils can indirectly be traced back to the lockstep character of American education.

The average public school teacher, greatly handicapped by increasing amounts of paperwork, discipline problems, and administrative support for "social promotion," have allowed pupils who were lacking the basic reading and writing skills to pass from one grade to the next. Many teachers and administrators echoed that these pupils have at least twelve chances of being exposed to a competent, effective educator who takes pride in the fact that he or she knows how to produce learning and mental growth in young people. Unfortunately, many pupils have not encountered these effective educators in the public school systems, especially in large urban areas, and even previously enthusiastic teachers pass the responsibility of educating lower income, inner city youths to some other individuals and institutions.

Certainly not all public school teachers have refused to be held accountable for the academic failure of their pupils and as a result, many dedicated educators have left the public schools rather than continue to participate in the charade of urban public education. Some of these educators gained positions in private schools, while others started their own schools for the children of parents who could afford to pay twice for their children's education. Meanwhile, many of the young people forced to remain in the public institutions went through twelve years of "schooling" and were graduated, even though they could not write or read and understand the daily newspaper. Here again the lockstep character of American public education prevents meaningful change and improvement in these educational conditions.

The homogeneous system of public schooling in the United States developed and matured long before psychologists and educators were able to identify the different learning styles of children. As far as American public schools are concerned, all children who are not suffering from some type of learning disability should be motivated to learn primarily reading, writing, and mathematics the way that it is taught in any classroom in any public school in the local district. If the pupils are more interested in music, art, drama, or foreign language, rather than using this interest to improve their basic literacy and mathematical skills, most public schools set aside short periods of time during the school week when pupils could participate in these "educational frills." There is, of course, great heterogeneity in private schooling in the United States and children of the wealthy may attend progressive free schools, strict religious schools, or exclusive boarding schools with facilities for enhancing and sharpening many of the talents and abilities of young children. This proposal offers a possible way of bringing greater heterogeneity to elementary and secondary public education in the United States while at the same time guaranteeing the acquisition of basic reading and writing skills.

Did the integration of public schools in the 1950s and 1960s bring about positive changes in public education? The role of public school integration was to bring all groups together regardless of race, class, and economic status to experience equal and quality education across America. What we have seen fifty years after the 1954 Brown versus the Board of Education Class Action decision is a reverse in educational practices and more segregated public schools. Blacks, the poor, and children of color are now learning less in deplorable educational facilities in the inner cities where they are the majority of the population.

During the 1960's, the deteriorating educational conditions in many urban public school systems were exposed in the writings of Jonathan Kozol, James Haskins, Nat Hentoff, James Herndon, John Holt, and many others. Moreover, the federal government attempted to breathe new life into inner city public schools through the Equal Opportunity Grants, the ESEA Title I-IV programs, and several other "compensatory education" projects. However, there were several very real problems in the conceptualization and evaluations of these programs. Basically, they attempted to "compensate" for

189

what many educators believe were deficiencies in the background of many black and some white students in the public schools or tried to improve their academic skills in order that they could gain admission to college. The basic premise of many of these programs was that these students had to develop their reading, math, and language skills; and that there was little in the social or cultural background of these students which would assist them in achieving academically in white institutions of higher education. Some educators finally realized that they could use the background and knowledge these children brought with them to the public schools in their instruction, but the guidelines for these programs often did not emphasize this approach, and many educators were not aware of the potentialities of this technique. This is an example where educational institutions failed to adjust their curriculum to accommodate the diversity of the American society.

In evaluating these programs, however, it became clear that federal guidelines which outlined how a program was to function may or may not have been appropriate for operating the programs in various localities throughout the country. Thus when the government tried to evaluate the Head Start program, using the federal guidelines which had been drawn up by officials in Washington, D.C., the researchers concluded that these programs were not achieving the objectives which had been set forth. But it was also clearly demonstrated that the "objectives" of Head Start programs varied from city to city, and from district to district depending on the academic needs of the children in the local areas. A Head Start center in an economically depressed area of a city may be preparing pre-schoolers in "reading readiness;" while another center, in the same section of the city, may have as its primary objective informing the parents of the area of the need to send their children to the center. Once there at this second center, the children were instructed in much more basic areas, such as tying their shoes, the information to be given a policemen if they are lost, how to play and work with other children in groups and teams, etc. The point is that the "objectives" of Head Start centers were as varied as there were centers, but the federal evaluators were only interested in determining if these centers were following through on the federal "guidelines" handed down from Washington. This approach created a huge vacuum in trying to educate blacks and children of color. What is needed is federal support for local educational programs, traditional and alternative, which are achieving significant results with the school children in that local district. National programs with guidelines set forth by administrators and researchers in Washington, D.C. are not necessarily going to make a significant impact on the educational achievement of students in Seattle, Washington, Los Angeles, California, Boston, Massachusetts, Miami, Florida, Detroit, Michigan, Chicago, Illinois, Jackson, Mississippi, Memphis, Tennessee, Charlotte, North Carolina, Orlando, Florida, or even in parts of the District of Columbia. The sooner the federal officials realize this fact, the sooner federal funds will be put to use supporting local alternative programs that are working with children in these local areas.

"No Child Left Behind" Act of 2001 Title I: Improving the Academic Achievement of the Disadvantaged.

SEC. 1001. STATEMENT OF PURPOSE

The purpose of this title is to ensure that all children have a fair, equal, and significant opportunity to obtain a high-quality education and reach, at a minimum, proficiency on challenging state academic achievement standards and state academic assessments. This purpose can be accomplished by the following:

1. Ensuring that high-quality academic assessments, accountability systems, teacher preparation and training, curriculum, and instructional materials are aligned with challenging State academic standards so that students, teachers, parents, and administrators can measure progress against common expectations for student academic achievement;

2. Meeting the educational needs of low-achieving children in our Nation's highest-poverty schools, limited English

proficient children, migratory children, children with disabilities, Indian children, neglected or delinquent children, and young children in need of reading assistance

3. Closing the achievement gap between high- and low-performing children, especially the achievement gaps between minority and nonminority students, and between disadvantaged children and their more advantaged peers;

4. Holding schools, local educational agencies, and States accountable for improving the academic achievement of all students, and identifying and turning around low-performing schools that have failed to provide a high-quality education to their students, while providing alternatives to students in such schools to enable the students to receive a high-quality education;

5. Distributing and targeting resources sufficiently to make a difference to local educational agencies and schools where needs are greatest;

6. Improving and strengthening accountability, teaching, and learning by using State assessment systems designed to ensure that students are meeting challenging State academic achievement and content standards and increasing achievement overall, but especially for the disadvantaged;

7. Providing greater decision making authority and flexibility to schools and teachers in exchange for greater responsibility for student performance;

8. Providing children an enriched and accelerated educational program, including the use of school wide programs or additional services that increase the amount and quality of instructional time;

9. Promoting school wide reform and ensuring the access of children to effective, scientifically based instructional strategies and challenging academic content;

10. Significantly elevating the quality of instruction by providing staff in participating schools with substantial opportunities for professional development;

11. Coordinating services under all parts of this title with each other, with other educational services, and, to the extent feasible, with other agencies providing services to youth, children, and families; and

12. Affording parents substantial and meaningful opportunities to participate in the education of their children. Source: "http://www.nochildleftbehind"

A pamphlet titled "The Partnership", Training, Networking, and Technical Assistance produced by The Florida Partnership for Family Involvement and Education asked questions and gave advice about The Title I Program as follows:

Does Your Child Attend A Title I School?
If so, did you know that Title I is a federal program designed:

✓ Help children do better in school and receive skills to be successful

✓ Provide resources for children to help them achieve to their best potential.

✓ Encourage parents to be more involved in their children's education.

✓ Provide opportunities for more teachers and aides in school.

✓ Provide opportunities for smaller class sizes.

✓ Help schools to facilitate activities designed to promote family involvement.

How Can Schools and Parents Work Together?

✓ Have training sessions for parents and teachers on how to effectively and positively communicate with each other.

✓ Arrange to have parent/teacher conferences, P.T.A./P.T.O. meetings, and other events not just at school sites. Use the community library, YMCA, YWCA and other facilities allowing for flexible meeting times.

✓ Publicize the benefits of belonging to the P.T.A./P.T.O. and encourage others to join.

✓ Provide transportation to school events and meetings.

✓ Provide childcare for events and meetings that may be adult-oriented.

✓ Establish an easily accessible family center on the school campus.

✓ Provide a home/school liaison to assist in communication between families and teachers.

Have You Signed Your Compact?

The Title I Program has established an initiative for a teacher/parent/student compact which is used in all Title I Schools. This compact is an agreement that promotes positive communication and involves the teacher/parent, and student in taking responsibility for certain task it is NOT just another piece of paper! The three parties meet and discuss the compact, take responsibility for the listed tasks, and then sign the compact.

Some Tasks Parents Agree To:

✓ Ensure their child attend school.

✓ Monitor television time and content their child watches.

✓ Promote good study habits and provide an effective work environment.

✓ Attend school functions.

✓ Communicate with the teacher regularly.

✓ Show respect for the school, teacher, and child.

Some Tasks Students Agree To:

✓ Attend school and be prepared to learn.

✓ Always try to do his/her best.

✓ Obey school and bus rules.

✓ Complete assignments on time.

✓ Be kind, respectful, and caring to others.
✓ Show respect and appreciation for the teacher, principal and other school personnel.

Some Tasks Teachers Agree To:

✓ Help the child to be successful.
✓ Provide information to parents in a timely manner of the child's progress.
✓ Enforce school and classroom rules fairly and consistently.
✓ Demonstrate professional behavior and a positive attitude.
✓ Provide meaningful and challenging learning experiences for the child.
✓ Maintain open communication with the parent and child.

(The Partnership, 2000-2003).

In the June 18, 2003, issue of the South Carolina Black News Paper, in Columbia, South Carolina, Nisa Islam Muhammad wrote an article titled *"Black Children in Extreme Poverty Hits Record High."* In her opening story, she stated several scenarios about Black children living in poverty. Her first case was about a child name Jason Tyler. At the age of seven, Jason Tyler knew something was different about his life. His friends wore new tennis shoes and clothes to school. His clothes came from the thrift store. They talked about having games and toys he was scared to even ask his mother about. He knew her answer would be the same whenever he asked for something: "Boy, I hardly have money to feed you much less buy you something." What Jason didn't know was that he, his two sisters and brother are among the growing numbers of extremely poor Black children was at its highest level in 23 years, according to the Children's Defense Fund (CDF).

Nearly one million Black children in 2001 lived in a family with an annual income of less than half the federal poverty level (disposable income below $7,064 for a family of three, including food and housing benefits) the CDF says. Its president, Marian Wright Edelman, explained that these numbers are clear indicators that, as a country, we must invest in children now instead of passing irresponsible tax breaks for the rich. It is shameful that one million Black children are left behind in extreme poverty," said Edelman. "It is hard to be poor. It is harder to be an extremely poor Black child in America when our president, who says we should "Leave No Child Behind," is proposing massive new tax breaks for the richest Americans."

Kesha Watson doesn't really understand or care about tax cuts. What she does know is that she doesn't have enough money to take care of her children. "I had a job, but I got laid off. Now I just work part-time and it's real hard. I can't afford day care for my 2-year-old. I can't find a job and it's getting harder and harder to make it," she told The Final-Call, the Black Muslim's newspaper. Her situation was further complicated by the Bush Administration's plans to dismantle Head Start, block grant Medicaid, as well as the Children's Health Insurance Program. Bush also wants to slash and /or freeze crucial services designed to help these poorest children.

While research shows that overall poverty has declined among Black children, it fails to highlight the plight or the record-breaking increase of children living in "extreme" poverty. "Poverty adds an additional hurdle for these students to overcome in reaching educational success. Being poor is one thing but being extremely poor makes success increasingly difficult. Something as simple and inexpensive as school supplies becomes an issue. They may come at the beginning of the year but they dwindle as the year progresses," says Valerie Butler, who teaches school in Houston, Texas. "No one wants to be stigmatized as being poor so these children try to compensate for what they lack. They still want the same things that others teens want, but it's just harder for them to get it. They may be poor, but any money they get is used for the things that will normalize their life like Nike tennis shoes and the latest music CDs."

CDF's analysis further shows that safety nets for the worst-off families, such as government assistance, are being eroded by government policies, which cause fewer extremely poor children of all races to receive cash and in-kind assistance that could help. The Bush Administration claims its plan to dismantle, eliminate, cut and freeze essential services for children to pay for massive new tax cuts that opponents claim are for the wealthiest Americans.

The Economic Report of the President, which the president's own Council of Economic Advisers issued in February 2003, explicitly acknowledges that tax cuts are unlikely to pay for investments in children and working families. "I don't know that if we can go across the globe to liberate Iraq, something needs to be done to liberate me and my children from this poverty," said Watson (Muhammad, 2003).

Author John F. Jennings, wrote an extensive article for Phi Delta Kappan Magazine in the March 2000, issue titled: Title I: *Its Legislative History and its Promise.* He stated the following:

In the United States, although state governments have primary responsibility for elementary and secondary education, the federal government provides significant but limited support in a few key areas. A special concern of the federal government for more than three decades has been the education of children who come to school with disadvantages-be they educational, economic, physical, or mental.

Title I of the Elementary and Secondary Education Act (ESEA) of 1965, is the principal embodiment of the national commitment to help educate economically and educationally disadvantaged children. This legislation has been regularly authorized for periods of five years and expired in the 1999-2000 congressional sessions. Thus, the President and Congress will have to decide whether and how to continue providing financial support to states and local school districts through Title I. In other words, they must ask themselves, is the education of disadvantaged children still a matter of national concern?

Although federal support for education is secondary to state support, it nevertheless has been important from the very beginnings of the nation. In the late 18th century, Congress encouraged the establishment of schools by setting aside land for their support -- in fact, a vast amount of land, 77 million acres. After the Civil War, Congress demanded that all new states admitted to the union provide free, nonsectarian public schools. During the 20th century, the federal government encouraged general support of schools and colleges by allowing federal income tax deductions, by promoting vocational education to train workers, by enacting the GI Bill of Rights, and by passing the National Defense Education Act to support science and mathematics instruction.

Over the course of two centuries, the federal government took action, although limited, in the area of education when vital national interests were involved -- supporting democracy by educating ordinary citizens in common schools and colleges; furthering economic prosperity by training workers; and providing for the defense of the nation by ensuring the health of children, their preparation in crucial areas of learning, and their training for jobs. These same objectives were behind the enactment of Title I of the ESEA and other legislation of the 1960s, designed to improve the education of disadvantaged children. But two additional imperatives for national action were also present: civil rights and social welfare.

In 1954, the U.S. Supreme Court in Brown vs. Board of Education ruled that segregation of children by race in the public schools was a violation of the 14th Amendment. That ruling gave rise to a national debate about the quality of education being provided to African American children and eventually led to a broader discussion of the needs of children of all races who came from poor families or who had other disadvantages.

When President John Kennedy assumed office in 1961, he proposed large-scale federal aid to improve education, including the education of Black children and of other poor and disadvantaged youths. At the time, Black children constituted approximately 13% of the enrollment in elementary and secondary schools. As a group, they were overwhelmingly poor -- 65% of Black children were living in poverty, compared with 20% of white children. In other words, the issues of race and poverty became linked because the facts of race and poverty in America were intertwined.

Most of President Kennedy's legislative proposals for education were not enacted because of three major obstacles. First, Southerners feared that, if schools received new federal aid to education, it would lead to forced integration of white and Black students. Second, conservatives said that new federal aid would lead to federal control of elementary and secondary education. Third, proponents of Catholic schools and other private schools blocked any new legislation that did not involve some aid to their schools.

In 1964, President Lyndon Johnson, who had assumed office after the assassination of President Kennedy, signed the Civil Rights Act, which sought to remove legal barriers to the full participation of blacks in American society. That law addressed one obstacle to federal school aid by signaling to the Southerners in Congress that the issue of integration had far broader implications than just education and would have to be dealt with one way or another.

In November 1964, Johnson was elected President by an overwhelming margin, and the electorate gave him a large Democratic majority in Congress. With this cushion of votes, Johnson was able to forge solutions to the remaining two major obstacles to new federal school aid. Earlier that year, Johnson had appointed a commission on education, chaired by John Gardner, president of the Carnegie Corporation, which recommended that federal aid not be general in nature but rather be targeted to particular categories of need. The commission suggested tying education aid to the new War on Poverty, which had been launched in the previous year. Johnson adopted this approach, and the ESEA proposed Title I as a program of aid to disadvantaged children, along with other "categorical" programs for the purchase of library books, the creation of supplemental education centers, and the development of state departments of education.

The vast bulk of the new funding was earmarked for Title I. Johnson's proposal built on the recommendation of Gardner's commission to tie aid to poverty by creating a "child benefit theory" of assistance. That is, federal money would "follow the disadvantaged child" to whatever school he or she attended -- public or private. But a "public trustee" would have to administer the funds for all such children, and that trustee would almost always be the local public school district. This compromise -- child-orientation but with public control of the funds -- cleared the way for Congress to pass the ESEA. The National Education Association withdrew its objections and endorsed the compromise, as did the U.S. Catholic Conference, the leading proponent of aid to private schools.

As for the last obstacle, fear of national control over education, Johnson had enough votes in 1965, to override the objections of the conservatives in Congress who raised that specter. But the legislation (P.L. 89-10, sect. 604) also addressed their concern directly by explicitly prohibiting federal control.

The ESEA of 1965, became the centerpiece of President Johnson's efforts to improve the lot of poor and Black youngsters, and the Title I program was the crown jewel of the ESEA. So important was this initiative to Johnson that he prevailed upon the House of Representatives to pass his bill with few changes. He then persuaded the Senate to accept it with no changes. All of this occurred in just 89 days through tremendous pressure from a powerful and committed President.

In the years after 1965, additional education laws were passed that built on the idea of categorical aid to provide extra assistance for children with disadvantages -- migrant children, children for whom English was a second language, delinquent and neglected children, and children with mental and physical handicaps. Frequently, the federal legislation was preceded or accompanied by lawsuits challenging the quality of education being provided to -- in some cases denied to -- these same groups of children. For instance, prior to the passage of the Education for All Handicapped Children Act in 1975, several state supreme courts had required the schools to admit children with mental and physical handicaps. In 1974, the

U.S. Supreme Court ruled in Lau v. Nichols that Chinese American children in San Francisco had been unconstitutionally denied an adequate education because they were taught only in English, a language they did not speak.

Thus upholding the Constitution was one of the vital national interests involved in the enactment of Title I and other programs for disadvantaged children, Black children, and disabled children. Children who spoke a limited amount of English were being denied their right to an adequate education under the 14th Amendment. A related motive was a strong concern about social welfare: many of these children were from poor families, and the problems stemming from poverty in American society ranked high on the national agenda in the 1960s. Constitutional and social welfare interests are the foundation stones on which all federal efforts to help educate disadvantaged children are built.

In the 1960s and 1970s, policy makers, educators, and other advocates for aid to disadvantaged children had high expectations for all these programs. They believed that the nation could wage a War on Poverty and that victory would mean the eradication of economic and other disadvantages. They accepted the idea that the "cycle of poverty" could be broken and that, with assistance, the poor would move into the middle class. But some thirty years later, the poor are still poor and many researchers would say that the poor are even poorer today.

Particularly high hopes were placed on the Title I program. In adopting Title I, Congress endorsed the idea that additional financial resources could make a difference in the education of poor and educationally disadvantaged Black children and simultaneously recognized the fact that concentrations of poverty have an adverse impact on the ability of school districts to provide such aid. Much less clear at that time was the matter of which types of educational services should be provided to poor and educationally disadvantaged children and by what means.

Consequently, the ESEA distributed the new financial resources to school districts according to the numbers of poor children enrolled, but it did not specify the types of services that districts should provide to "educationally deprived" children. This approach showed both a deference to local control -- an answer to critics who feared federal control of curriculum -- and a prevailing belief that the main shortcoming was a lack of funding, not a lack of knowledge about better ways to educate disadvantaged Black children (Jennings 2000 ¶ 1-18).

John Jennings continued his assessment of the federal government's role in supporting elementary and secondary education by the stating the following comments:

The basic issue that the President and Congress must address in their review of Title I and related programs is whether it is still in the national interest to work to ensure a good education for economically and educationally disadvantaged children. Over the course of two centuries of American history, the federal government has become involved in education when a national interest has been identified.

When the federal government determines that an issue in education is of national importance, then financial assistance usually follows. This means that states, school districts, colleges and universities, and students receive funding and services. However, the identification of a national interest in education is of far greater importance than the amount of federal financial assistance that this attracts. Focusing the national spotlight on a problem invariably spurs governors, state legislators, boards of education, and other policy makers to address the same issue. For example, the national action to develop Title I and the other programs in the 1960s and 1970s, led to many state and local actions to address the obstacles facing children with economic and educational disadvantages and physical and mental disabilities. Therefore, the broader question that must be addressed is, are the problems facing disadvantaged Black children still of sufficient national importance to warrant federal action and state and local attention?

In 1960, 27% of American children lived in poverty. That proportion declined to 15% in the early 1970s, partly as a result of the War on Poverty programs. Unfortunately, the number of poor children has crept back up, and 20% of all children today come from low-income families. In the future, the nation's growth in population is projected to be among the racial and ethnic groups with high rates of poverty. Clearly, the poor are still with us and constitute a substantial proportion of the populations served in our elementary and secondary schools.

Moreover, the strong correlation between children's success in school and their families' income level still holds. Thus the number of poor children in American schools continues to present the nation with a difficult challenge, especially if raising the educational achievement of all children continues to be the nation's goal.

Finally, there remains a disparity between the educational achievement of African American students and the student population as a whole. Many African American children remain in inner-city and poor rural school districts, which are too frequently not offering them an education of high -- or even good -- quality. The dissolution of federal court orders requiring the busing of school children to achieve integration will in all likelihood lead to further racial isolation. Children of Hispanic origin are also becoming increasingly concentrated in schools with children who share their ethnic background, and Hispanic children are fast becoming the largest disadvantaged people of color in American schools.

These facts mean that the constitutional and social welfare rationales that in the 1960s prompted the creation of programs of federal aid for disadvantaged children are still valid today. The other reasons that spurred the federal government to support education in the past are also still present -- the need to promote democracy, strengthen national defense, and improve the skills of the work force.

During the 30-year history of Title I, debates took place about whether the program was too restrictive or too loose, whether the emphasis ought to be on serving children in the highest concentrations of poverty or on reaching all disadvantaged and Black children, and whether the focus ought to be on fiscal or educational accountability. In a way, these were all arguments over the details of our national commitment to raising the educational achievement of disadvantaged black children. For those three decades, most Presidents, members of Congress, educators, and citizens shared a broad agreement that it was in the national interest to make a major effort to address the needs of disadvantaged Black children.

During 1999-2000, legislative session, Congress and the President considered whether there is still a national interest in improving the education of disadvantaged and Black children. Since that period has passed, national leaders must reaffirm our country's commitment to raising the educational achievement of disadvantaged and Black children. Any other result would not be true to the facts or to American history, and any other course would not be in the best economic, social, and moral interests of the country (Jennings, 2000, ¶ 23-31).

The role of federal government in assisting parents in rearing their children is one of great national interest. The federal government reassures all parents that provisions will be made to be sure that no child is left behind. Just think what our public education systems would look like today if the federal government hadn't intervened in providing legal assistance and funding for public school districts throughout this country. If we think our public schools are in disarray today, you can just imagine if local and state governments had total control over the governance of public education; poor, Black, and children of color would suffer more than they are suffering now, and they will truly be left behind.

As long as our country has "A government of the people, by the people, and for the people," then our looking out for our country is actually looking out for ourselves. Indeed, patriotism is a vital condition of both national and personal security. But blind patriotism is no real patriotism at all, just sanctified loyalty gone mad, so, I would never say, "my country right or wrong," but would rather say, "my country when right, keep it right; when wrong, set it right." That's true patriotism. It builds a country worth building and keeps a country worth keeping. It puts together the elements of a civilized society worthy to be transmitted to our children. This should be the true role of the Federal Government in assisting parents with rearing their children in the 21st century.

Summary

Hopefully, this book serves as some assistance to all of us who have an interest in helping to rear children. As long as we have human beings, we will always have our children. By rearing strong, productive, and educated children, we reassure our future. This is an investment from which we all will benefit. Always remember, there is no such thing as being a perfect parent, grandparent, significant family member, or having perfect children.

There is no one way in rearing children, because children respond differently to different modes of child rearing. My advice to parents in the child bearing stages, is to try to have more than one child. Having siblings teaches children a lot of necessary life skills, like sharing, getting along with people who are different, cooperation, problem solving, and responsibility. Usually, parents who have more than one child don't have time to spoil just one child because parents have to share their time between the children. This guidebook has suggested strategies and recommendations for parental involvement in children's growth and development.

Parent by parent, youth by youth, voter by voter, professional by professional, congregation by congregation, club by club, community by community, corporation by corporation, city by city, county by county, state by state- all Americans have a moral, personal, and professional obligation to ensure that no child is left behind.

Appendix I

Samples of
Parents, Teachers, Staff, Directors and Administrators Seminar and Workshop Evaluations
(2004-2006)

WORKSHOP EVALUATION

To help us assess the effectiveness of this Conference, please take a few minutes to complete the following evaluation.

Presenter: Dr. Willie J. Kimmons   Presentation Title _Save Our Children / Save Our Schools_

1. This workshop was extremely helpful because... _it brings the "real"_ _to life_

2. I would like to see more/less of ... _parents involved in their_ _Children's lives!_

3. When I return to my school site, I will ... _spread the word._ _Encourage persons to "save our children._

4.	The content was clear and well organized.	(Excellent)	Good	Fair	Poor
5.	The presenter provided new viewpoints/issues.	(Excellent)	Good	Fair	Poor
6.	The presenter was well prepared.	(Excellent)	Good	Fair	Poor

7. What did you like best, or find most useful about this presentation?
Powerful testimonies

8. What would you like Dr. Kimmons to do differently?
Be a Keynote Speaker, he needs _a longer time to_

Additional Comments:

> **DR. WILLIE J. KIMMONS**
> Career Educator, Former College
> President, Teacher, Educational
> Consultant for Pre-K-16 Schools. Title
> I Parents, Teachers, Students and
> Motivational Speaker

Thank you for your cooperation.

Name (optional) _____
Position _RVI Coordinator (Work Preparedness for Special Needs Coord.)_
City/State _Atlanta GA_
Date _3/8/06_

210

WORKSHOP EVALUATION

To help us assess the effectiveness of this Conference, please take a few minutes to complete the following evaluation.

Presenter: Dr. Willie J. Kimmons   Presentation Title _Parental Influence on Quality Instruction_

1. This workshop was extremely helpful because...

Speaker is knowledgeable, insightful + motivational

2. I would like to see more/less of ...

3. When I return to my school site, I will ...

Suggest that principal contact speaker to make a presentation for our faculty/staff

4. The content was clear and well organized.	(Excellent)	Good	Fair	Poor
5. The presenter provided new viewpoints/issues.	(Excellent)	Good	Fair	Poor
6. The presenter was well prepared.	(Excellent)	Good	Fair	Poor

7. What did you like best, or find most useful about this presentation?

Real life examples / application

8. What would you like Dr. Kimmons to do differently?

Additional Comments:

Great job!

DR. WILLIE J. KIMMONS
Career Educator, Former College
President, Teacher, Educational
Consultant for Pre-K-16 Schools, Title I
Parents. Teachers, Students and
Motivational Speaker

Thank you for your cooperation.

Name (optional) _CHIQUITA POLITE_

Position _TEACHER_

City/State _AUGUSTA, GA_

Date _3/9/06_

211

Parent Workshop
6pm — 8pm
Evaluation

Recovation Academy
Memphis City School
FEB 16 2006

DR. WILLIE J. KIMMONS, Consultant/Presenter
"SAVE OUR CHILDREN, SAVE OUR SCHOOLS — NEVER, EVER GIVE UP ON OUR CHILDREN"

1. What did you like best, or what did you find most useful about this presentation?

That he used personal experiences to relate to the audience.
He used encouraging words to the students.

2. What would you like Dr. Kimmons to do differently? Nothing!

I think he is dynamic!!!

3. How will you use the information presented?

By telling others about Dr. Kimmons, about the topics, and how he motivated the audience.

4. Additional comments:

I think he is very credible. I have the utmost respect for him. I wish "God's riches Blessings" upon him!!!

Full Gospel Tabernacle
789 State Rd 38116

Name (optional) Minister Betty J. Negrew
Position Minister   Phone (901) 396-4795

212

DATE *October 20, 2005*

WORKSHOP EVALUATION

Please complete and submit at the conclusion of the presentation. Thank you!!

DR. WILLIE J. KIMMONS, Consultant/Presenter
"SAVE OUR CHILDREN, SAVE OUR SCHOOLS — NEVER, EVER GIVE UP ON OUR CHILDREN"

1. What did you like best, or what did you find most useful about this presentation?

He delivered his information in a Simply form with great impact

2. What would you like Dr. Kimmons to do differently?

NOTHING!

3. How will you use the information presented?

I will use this information as a tool for the continuing challenges of parenting.

4. Additional comments:

Thanks for your excellent presentation.

Name (optional) *LaTerra Floyd Battle*

Position *Elementary School* Phone *770-498-6842*
Instructional Support Staff

213

Evaluation

DR. WILLIE J. KIMMONS, Consultant/Presenter
"SAVE OUR CHILDREN, SAVE OUR SCHOOLS --- NEVER, EVER GIVE UP ON OUR CHILDREN"

1. What did you like best, or what did you find most useful about this presentation?

The Dr.s presentation was very motivational and energetic

2. What would you like Dr. Kimmons to do differently?

3. How will you use the information presented?

I will share it with the teachers and use it with the fathers

4. Additional comments:

He made me feel better and gave me confidence.

Name (optional) Victor M Corona

Position Male and Father Initiative Phone

214

Evaluation

Jan. 10, 2006

DR. WILLIE J. KIMMONS, Consultant/Presenter
"SAVE OUR CHILDREN, SAVE OUR SCHOOLS --- NEVER, EVER GIVE UP ON OUR CHILDREN"

1. What did you like best, or what did you find most useful about this presentation?

It was very informative. I am glad to have been here.

2. What would you like Dr. Kimmons to do differently?

Not a thing. He spoke very well.

3. How will you use the information presented?

I will share it with family. Especially my daughter.

4. Additional comments:

It's been a pleasure having met and listened to Dr. Kimmons

Name (optional) Miguel Ferrer

Position _____ Phone 863-634-0634

215

Jan. 18, 2006

Evaluation

DR. WILLIE J. KIMMONS, Consultant/Presenter
"SAVE OUR CHILDREN, SAVE OUR SCHOOLS — NEVER, EVER GIVE UP ON OUR CHILDREN"

1. What did you like best, or what did you find most useful about this presentation?

THE EMPHASIS ON PATIENCE, COMPASSION & TOLERANCE.
FOCUSING ON STRENGTHENING ONES SPIRIT IN
ORDER TO BE PATIENT & TOLERANT.
ENDURING NEGATIVE BEHAVIOR TO SEE A
POSITIVE OUTCOME. (FINDING THE NICHE)

2. What would you like Dr. Kimmons to do differently?

WIN THE NOBEL PRIZE.
SERIOUSLY!

3. How will you use the information presented?

EVERYDAY - AT HOME, IN THE
COMMUNITY, AT WORK AND IN
MINISTERING TO OTHERS

4. Additional comments: "FATHER IN HEAVEN, BY THE COVENANT OF YOUR WORDS:
"SUFFER THE LITTLE CHILDREN TO COME UNTO ME, HE WHO WOULD HARM THE LEAST
OF THESE, IT WOULD BE BETTER TO TIE A MILLSTONE AROUND THEIR NECK AND
CAST THEMSELVES INTO THE SEA." - BIND ALL EVIL ATTACKING OUR CHILDREN
AND THEIR PARENTS, TEACHERS & GUARDIANS. MANIFEST IN THIS SEASON VICTORY
IN THIS WAR FOR THE SOULS, MIND & BODIES OF OUR CHILDREN. ANOINT US
WITH YOUR PROTECTION, REMOVE THE FOG OF CONFUSION, REBELLION, DISRESPECT
FROM ALL OF OUR MINDS. RENEW US LORD JESUS. IN YOUR HOLY NAME
AMEN

Name (optional) Ronald A. Johnson MFA

Position ART DIRECTOR / TEACHER   Phone 901- 859-4585 · CELL
                                          916·1030 Ext 31458 WK

216

Oct, 10, 2005

Evaluation

DR. WILLIE J. KIMMONS, Consultant/Presenter
"SAVE OUR CHILDREN, SAVE OUR SCHOOLS --- NEVER, EVER GIVE UP ON OUR
CHILDREN"

1. What did you like best, or what did you find most useful about this presentation?

I liked best the enthusiasm and personality of Dr. Kimmons. He made it so realistic!! He kept our attention!

2. What would you like Dr. Kimmons to do differently?

Nothing.

3. How will you use the information presented?

Personally and Professionally

4. Additional comments:

We need more men & speakers like Dr. Kimmons

Name (optional) Juanita Jones
Position Policy Council   Phone 6623759960

217

Evaluation

Nov. 17, 2005

DR. WILLIE J. KIMMONS, Consultant/Presenter
"SAVE OUR CHILDREN, SAVE OUR SCHOOLS --- NEVER, EVER GIVE UP ON OUR CHILDREN"

1. What did you like best, or what did you find most useful about this presentation?

Everything he said will be very useful in raising my 2 children. Ages 4 and 2½

2. What would you like Dr. Kimmons to do differently?

Nothing

3. How will you use the information presented?

In raising my children.

4. Additional comments:

This was a wonderful presentation.

Name (optional) *Mercy Ojeda*
Position *Parent Volunteer*   Phone (___) 593-5___

218

Evaluation

Dec. 16, 2005

DR. WILLIE J. KIMMONS, Consultant/Presenter
"SAVE OUR CHILDREN, SAVE OUR SCHOOLS --- NEVER, EVER GIVE UP ON OUR CHILDREN"

1. What did you like best, or what did you find most useful about this presentation?

Powerful! Great stories!

2. What would you like Dr. Kimmons to do differently?

3. How will you use the information presented?

For Sure!

4. Additional comments:

Thank you for advocating for children!

Name (optional) Marcia Lucero Kitzmiller
Position Teacher   Phone 505·267-8270

219

FEB 15, 2006

Evaluation

DR. WILLIE J. KIMMONS, Consultant/Presenter
"SAVE OUR CHILDREN, SAVE OUR SCHOOLS — NEVER, EVER GIVE UP ON OUR CHILDREN"

1. What did you like best, or what did you find most useful about this presentation?

    Dr Kimmons is a very powerful speaker. I enjoyed this session for all the information and motivation.

2. What would you like Dr. Kimmons to do differently?

    Nothing, Just keep doing what your doing. God Bless!

3. How will you use the information presented?

    I purchased a book and will share it with my school.

4. Additional comments:

    I loved this session and am very happy that I attended. Thank you and God Bless!

Name (optional) _Raline Schott_

Position _Kindergarten teacher_ Phone _(509) 491-3208_
& Head Start Parent

220

DATE 12.1.05

WORKSHOP EVALUATION

Please complete and submit at the conclusion of the presentation. Thank you!!

DR. WILLIE J. KIMMONS, Consultant/Presenter
"SAVE OUR CHILDREN, SAVE OUR SCHOOLS — NEVER, EVER GIVE UP ON OUR CHILDREN"

1. What did you like best, or what did you find most useful about this presentation?

The speaker was great

2. What would you like Dr. Kimmons to do differently?

3. How will you use the information presented?

To become a better Dad

4. Additional comments:

Good Job
I was taught something today.
This is needed more today.

Name (optional)_____

Position _____Phone_____

221

Evaluation

DR. WILLIE J. KIMMONS, Consultant/Presenter
"SAVE OUR CHILDREN, SAVE OUR SCHOOLS — NEVER, EVER GIVE UP ON OUR
CHILDREN"

1. What did you like best, or what did you find most useful about this presentation?

Dr. Kimmons has such a powerful presence that you can't help but pay attention to what he is saying.

2. What would you like Dr. Kimmons to do differently?

Provide more hand-outs for parents.

3. How will you use the information presented?

I will use these checklists to refer back to in order to check myself and make sure that I am doing all that I can to help move my child forward!

4. Additional comments:

Excellent presentation! Enjoyed it very much.

Name (optional) Connie Ross Jan. 12, 2006
Position Parent   Phone (916) 722-0101

222

Evaluation

DR. WILLIE J. KIMMONS, Consultant/Presenter
"SAVE OUR CHILDREN, SAVE OUR SCHOOLS — NEVER, EVER GIVE UP ON OUR
CHILDREN"

1. What did you like best, or what did you find most useful about this presentation?

The presenter was excellent,
very informative, good sense
a humor.

2. What would you like Dr. Kimmons to do differently? Nothing

3. How will you use the information presented?

Become a better parent & mentor
to my children,
Encouragement!

4. Additional comments;

I ~~that ~~ ~~learned~~

Name (optional) Jy Figueroa April 6, 2006

Position Lay Advocate for Phone _____
the office of the Prosecuter

223

Evaluation

DR. WILLIE J. KIMMONS, Consultant/Presenter
"SAVE OUR CHILDREN, SAVE OUR SCHOOLS --- NEVER, EVER GIVE UP ON OUR CHILDREN"

1. What did you like best, or what did you find most useful about this presentation?

The way the Presenter presented such valuable information to our parents, staff and others.

2. What would you like Dr. Kimmons to do differently?

Nothing

3. How will you use the information presented?

As a resource for my parents in Head Start

4. Additional comments:

Presenter has a lot to offer especially for today's families, schools and communities — (with so many problems

Name (optional) *Roszeta F. Davis*   FEB, 16, 2006

Position *Family & Community*   Phone _____
Service Specialist — New Orleans, LA

224

Evaluation

DR. WILLIE J. KIMMONS, Consultant/Presenter
"SAVE OUR CHILDREN, SAVE OUR SCHOOLS --- NEVER, EVER GIVE UP ON OUR
CHILDREN"

1. What did you like best, or what did you find most useful about this presentation?

The presentation was most helpful in my raising of a 16 yr old male. It reinforced the role of parents as the first stage in the development of healthy/productive adults

2. What would you like Dr. Kimmons to do differently?

Everything was well presented

3. How will you use the information presented?

To continue to do my best as a parent.

4. Additional comments:

Thanks - most informative and well presented

Name (optional) *Deanne Coleman* MARCH 10, 2006

Position _____Phone_____

225

APPENDIX II

WHAT CHILDREN NEED FROM A TO Z

KIDS A B C'S

Approval	Naps
Brain Power	Openness
Caring	Play time
Discipline	Quiet time
Education	Restrictions
Friends	Security
Generosity	Truth
Hugs	Understanding
Instruction	Variety
Joy	Welcome
Kisses	eXercise
Love	Yearning
Mentors	Zeal

Dr. Willie J. Kimmons, Career Educator, Former College President.
Teacher, Educational Consultant for Pre-K-16 Schools, Title I Parents, Teachers,
Students, and Motivational Speaker

APPENDIX III

Things Money Can't Buy for Your Children

1. Praying with your child and attending church with him/her.

2. Sharing a first with a child.

3. Hugs for and from your child.

4. Talking with your child.

5. Listening to your child.

6. Supporting a child in your community.

7. True friends.

8. Being a good neighbor.

9. Walks with your child.

10. Participating in your child's work and life.

11. Attending your child's school and activities.

12. Reading to and with your child.

13. Telling your child that you love him/her and show it.

14. Spending time with your child.

15. Memories

16. Values

17. Happiness

18. Love of Learning

19. Experience and Exposure

20. Sense of Humor

Dr. Willie J. Kimmons, Career Educator, Former College President, Teacher, Educational Consultant for Pre-K-16 Schools, Title I Parents, Teachers, Students and Motivational Speaker

234

Other Books and Publications by Dr. Kimmons:

Black Administrators in Public Community Colleges: Self-Perceived Role and Status A Heartstone Book, Carlton Press Inc. (1977). New York, New York.

Sex: Yes, No, Maybe So The Sex Book Committee of The Student Personnel Services Division, North Carolina Central University (1974). Durham, North Carolina.

Teaching Our Children About The Realities of Life, A, B, C, & D's *The Daytona Times Newspaper.* (November, 2003). Daytona Beach, Florida.

The Status of African Americans, Poor People and People of Color After Dr. King's Death (two part series). *Daytona Times Newspaper.* February 5-11 and February 12-18, 2004, vol. XXVII No. 6, section B and vol. XXVII no. 7, section B.

Educating The Black Child For The 21st Century: Implications For Historically and Predominantly Black Colleges and Universities. *Black Issues in Higher Education.* (September 10, 1992). Fairfax, Virginia.

Bibliography

Botrie, Maureen, Wenger, Pat. (1992). Teachers and Parents Together. Markham, Ontario. Pembroke Publishers Limited/Stenhouse Publishers, Portland, ME.

Brownlow, Leroy (1989). Today and Forever. Fort Worth, Texas: Brownlow Publishing Company.

Bruce, Barbara. (1996). Seven Ways of Teaching The Bible to Children. Nashville, Tennessee: Abingdon Publishing Company.

Butler, E.D., Rev. Dr. The Family-Our Greatest Need-God. Sunday Sermon, Second Missionary Baptist Church. Bloomington, IN. March 5, 2000.

Carnegie Corporation of New York (1994). Starting Points: Meeting the Needs of our Youngest Children. New York, New York.

Carnegie Corporation of New York (1996). Years of Promise: A Comprehensive Learning Strategy for American's Children. New York, New York.

Clark, Faye & Frank 1998. They're All Our Children, and Their Crusade to Educate the Children: Educate the Children Foundation, New York, New York.

Clements, Mark, 16 May 1993. What's Wrong with Our Schools. Parade Magazine, New York, New York.

Comer, James P. and Poussaint, Alvin F. (1976). Black Child Care. New York, New York: Pocket Books, Simon and Schuster, Inc.

Cosby, William H. "Bill". (1998) Fatherhood. Garden City, New York: Doubleday Publishing Company.

Crosby, Margee S. 30 December 2000. Speech at the National Childcare Institute Conference, "The Imporant Role Parental Involvement Plays in Rearing Children of Color," Jacksonville, Florida.

Dobson, James, (1987). Dare to Discipline. Tyndale House Publishers, Wheaton, Il.

Donlevy, James G.; Donlevy, Tia Rice (1997)." Perspectives on Education And School Reform", International Journal of Instructional Media, v. 24 no3 ¶ 1-20). Retrieved from FirstSearch Database on May 13, 2003, "http://www. firstsearch@oclc.org"

Dreikurs, Rudolf, and Grey, Loren. (1970). A Parents' Guide to Child Discipline: A Modern System for Raising Modern Children New York, New York: Hawthorn Books, Inc.

DuCharme, Catherine Campbell, (1998). Education Magazine. V. 119 no2 (winter 1998) ChulaVista, California, ¶ 1-14). Retrieved from FirstSearch Database on May 13, 2003, "http://www.firstsearch.oclc.org"

Edelman, M. (1998). Children's Defense Fund. The State of America's Children. Washington, D.C.

Edelman, M. (1992). The Measure of Our Success: A Letter to My Children and Yours. Boston, MA: Beacon Press.

Edmonds, Ronald R. An Overview: Programs of School Improvement: Toward More Effective Schools. Educational Leadership. December 1982. vol. 40, n03. pp. 4-12

Excerpts from Report on the Seven Cardinal Principles of Secondary Education (1918). Are reprinted in John H. Best and Robert T. Sidwell, eds., The American Legacy Of Learning: Reading in the History of Education (Philadelphia, PA 1967), pp. 271-275.

Fantini, Mario D., <u>Alternative Education: A Source Book for Parents, Teachers, Students, Administrator</u> (New York, 1976). P. 9: see also, <u>Public Schools of Choice: A Plan For the Reform of American Education</u> (New York, 1974); and Special Issue: "Alternative Schools" <u>Harvard Education Review</u> 42 (August 1972): pp. 313-436.

Fege, Arnold F. (2000). <u>From Fun Raising to Hell Raising: New Roles for Parents</u> Educational Leadership, v. 57 no7 (April 2000), ¶. 1-43. Retrieved from FirstSearch database on May 13, 2003 "<u>http://www.firstsearch@oclc.org</u>"

For a detailed discussion and analysis of federal aid to various types of schools districts Throughout the United States, see, Alan L. Ginsburg and J. Neil Killalea. Killalea, "<u>Patterns of Federal Aid to School Districts</u>," <u>Journal of Education Finance</u> 2 (Winter 1977): pp. 380-395.

Hart, Peter D. (1999, November). <u>All for All: Strengthening Community Involvement For All Students.</u> Public Education Network, Washington, D.C.

Havens, Mark M., School Administrator (2001). <u>Beyond Money: Benefits Of An Education Foundation.</u> V.58 no7 (August 2001) ¶ 1-30). Retrieved from the WilsonSelectPlus database on May 13, 2003 "<u>http://www.wilsonselectplus@oclc.org</u>"

Jennings, John F. "Title I: Its Legislative History and its Promise." Phi Delta Kappan v.81 no. 7. (March 2000) ¶ 23-31 Retrieved from the FirstSearch database on May 13, 2003. "<u>http://www. firstsearch.org</u>"

Kozol, Jonathan, <u>Death At An Early Age</u> (New York, 1967); James Haskins, <u>Diary of a Harlem School Teacher</u> (New York, 1969); Nat Henthoff, <u>Our Children Are Dying</u> (New York, 1966); James Herndon, <u>The Way It Spozed to Be</u> (New York, 1968); John Holt, <u>How Children Fail</u> (New York, 1967); Herbert Kohl, <u>36 Children</u> (New York, 1967).

Kozol, Jonathan (1991). <u>Savage Inequalities: Children in America's Schools</u>. Harper- Perennial. New York, New York.

Ladson-Billings, G. (1994). <u>The Dream Keepers: Successful Teachers of African American Children.</u> San Francisco, CA: Jossey-Bass Publishers.

Langston, Teresa (1993). <u>Parenting Without Pressure, A Parent's Guide</u>. NAV Press, Colorado Springs, CO.

Levine, Arthur E. (1996) p. 7. Annual Report of the College, Teachers College, New York, New York.

Love, Mary A. (2002). <u>Flex: Focus on Learning for an Effective Educational Ministry For Christ.</u> Charlotte, North Carolina: Love's Creative Resources.

Masterson, Kathryn. <u>States Fret Paying for Schools. Law No Child Left Behind: Strains Budgets. </u>The Daytona Beach News Journal, May 2003.

McDonough, Siobhan (2003) <u>Study Reveals Top Education Concerns.</u> Washington Post, 23 April 2003. Washington, D.C.

Mendler, Allen N. and Curwin, Richard L. (1999). <u>Discipline with Dignity For Challenging Youth.</u> Bloomington, Indiana: National Educational Service.

Muhammad, Nisa, Islam (June 12 & 18, 2003). <u>Black Children in Extreme Poverty Hits Record High.</u>. South Carolina Black News Paper. Columbia, South Carolina.

National School Boards Association. (1998, May 12). <u>Retired Couple Creates Foundation To Help Impoverished Schools</u>. School Board News, 18(12), 8.

No Child Left Behind Act of 2001. Title I: <u>Improving the Academic Achievement of the Disadvantaged,</u> 107th Congress 1st Session. Prepared by the National Clearinghouse for

Bilingual Education, The George Washington University, 13 December 2001.

O'Connor, Grace. (1966). Helping Your Children: A Basic Guide for Parents. Austin, Texas: Steck-Vaughn Company.

Paige, Rod.(April 8, 2002). Schools Can't Improve Without Help of Parents. Retrieved from the Worldwide Web, USA Today, 7 June 2002. "http://www.usatoday.com"

Paige, Rod The Facts: Raising Achievement For African Americans. Retrieved From The Worldwide wed 19 June 2002. "http://www.nochildleftbehind.gov"

Parenting. (2003). The Parenting Group Magazine. New York, New York. February, Issue.

Parents and Children Together. Family Literacy Center. (1991 & 1992) Bloomington, Indiana: Indiana University.

Public Agenda Associated Press (2000). Aches in Education. Washington, D.C.

Puriefoy, Wendy D. (1999 Nov.) All for All: Strengthening Community Involvement for All Students. President, Public Education Network, Washington, D.C. "Hschaffer@PublicEducation.org"

Quint, S. (1994). Schooling Homeless Children: A Working Model for American's Public Schools. New York: Teachers College press.

Ratner, Gary, States Must be Given Road Map to Assure No Child Will Be Lost. The Daytona Beach News Journal. 3 February 2003. Daytona Beach, FL

Reaching All Families: Creating Family-Friendly Schools, Beginning of the School Year Activities. Office of Educational Research and Improvements. (2000) Washington, D.C.: U.S. Department of Education.

Reaching For Excellence: <u>An Effective Schools Source Book</u>. (1985). Washington, D.C.: The National Institute of Education: U.S. Department of Education. May Issue.

Rohn, Charles (2001 May-June<u>). Plenty of Religious Expression in Public Schools</u>. Illinois School Board Journal.

Schorr, L. (1988). <u>Within Our Reach: Breaking the Cycle of Disadvantage</u>, New York: New York. Anchor Press/ Doubleday.

Schultz, Theodore, "Education and Economic Growth," in <u>The Sixtieth Yearbook of the National Society for the Study of Education</u>, Part II, "Social Forces Influencing American Education," Nelson Henry, editor (Chicago, 1961); see also, T. Schultz, <u>The Economic Value of Education</u> (New York, 1963); and Nicholas Georgescu-Roegen, "Economics and Educational Development," <u>Journal of Education Finance 2</u> (Summer 1976): 1-15.

<u>The Florida Partnership for Family Involvement in Education:</u> A Project of FND of The Partnership 2000-2003.

The Parent Institute: Quick Tips. (2002). <u>Parents are Teachers, Too!</u> Fairfax Station, Virginia.

Watch Tower Bible and Tract Society of BrooklynNew York, (1996). <u>The Secret of Family Happiness.</u> International Bible Students Association, Publishers.

Wolk, R.A. & Rodman, B.H.(1994). <u>Classroom Crusaders</u>. San Francisco, CA: Jossey-Bass Publishers.

Woyshner, Christine. <u>Race, Gender, and the Early PTA: Civic Engagement and Public Education, 1897-1924</u>. Teacher's College Record Vol. 105 n03. April, 2003, ¶ 1-6. New York, New York. Retrieved from FirstSearch Database on May 13, 2003, <u>"http://www.firstsearch@ocl.org"</u>

Young, Jeffrey R. Black Students Lack Mentors in Schools. <u>Chronicle of Higher Education.</u> 31 January, 2003. Washington, D.C.

Dr. Kimmons has served at every level in the higher education teaching and learning process with dedication and distinction. He has been a classroom teacher, college professor, dean, vice president, interim president, campus president and Chancellor for two and four year colleges and universities. Currently, he is serving as an Educational Consultant for Pre-K-16 schools, working with parents and teachers of Title I schools, and he is also a motivational speaker.

He has given more than 500 presentations and lectures to all types of organizations including, Chambers of Commerce, religious organizations, Kiwanis, Rotary and Lions clubs, NAACP, Urban League, economic development organizations, political groups, Greek organizations, youth groups, parenting conferences, workshops, and other community organizations. Dr. Kimmons currently serves as a nationwide spokesperson and proposal reviewer for diabetes, breast and prostate cancer and other health related matters. He serves on the African American Men's Health Summit Steering Committee for Prostate Cancer of Central Florida. Dr. Kimmons serves on more than 10 different community boards and advisory councils in the city of Daytona Beach and the county of Volusia, Florida. In addition, he has served as a mentor and volunteer in public schools in Daytona Beach/Volusia County, Florida for the past four years.